D1027814

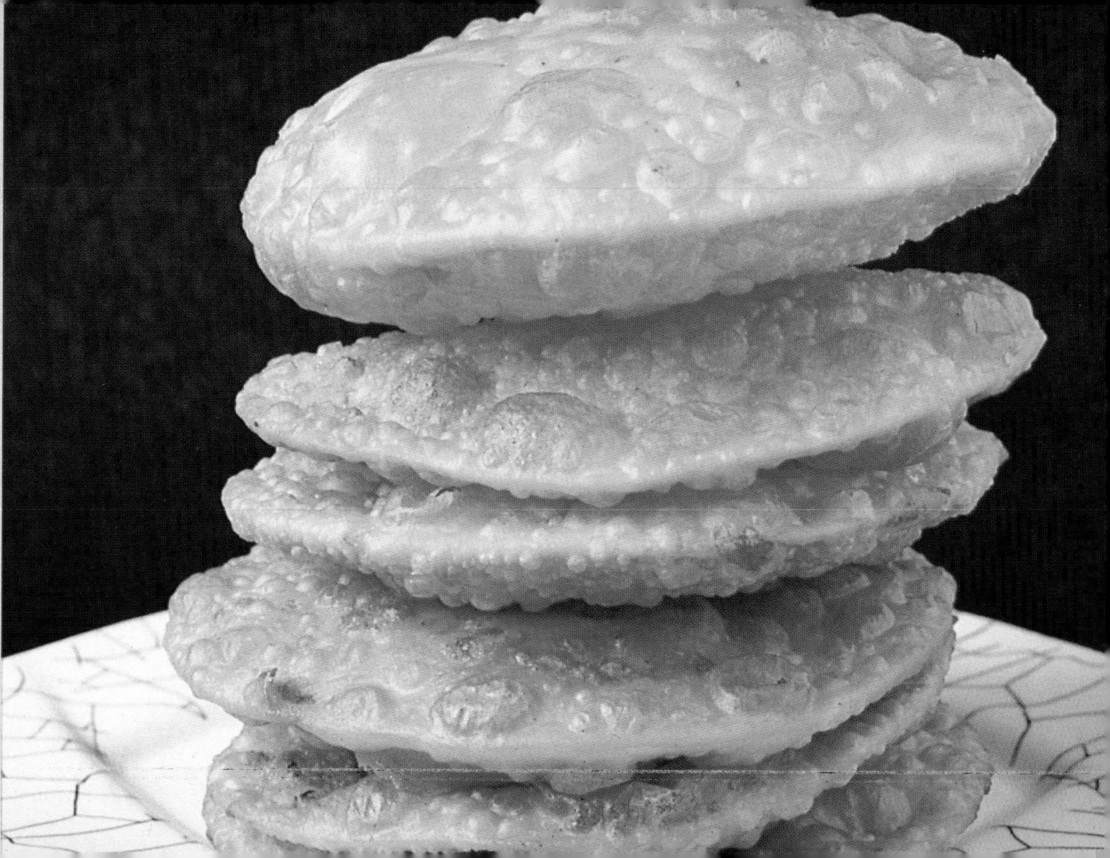

Urad Dal Ki Kachori

SANJEEV KAPOOR'S
SIMPLY VEGETARIAN
Recipes for the Indian Kitchen
Snacks & Starters II

SANJEEV KAPOOR'S
SIMPLY VEGETARIAN
Recipes for the Indian Kitchen

Snacks & Starters II

In association with Alyona Kapoor

Popular
prakashan

POPULAR PRAKASHAN PVT. LTD.

© 2005 by Sanjeev Kapoor

First Published 2004

(3884)

ISBN - 81-7991-136-5

PRINTED IN INDIA
By International Print-O-Pac Ltd
C-4 to 11, Ph - II, Extension, Noida, (UP)
and Published by Ramdas Bhatkal
for Popular Prakashan Pvt. Ltd.

Exclusive Distributors :
Impulse Marketing
G-43, IInd Floor, Green Park Main Market
New Delhi - 110 016.
Ph.: 91-11-26526663, 26526664, Fax: 91-11- 26562171

Dedication

To all the lovers of authentic
food whose enthusiasm makes us
dig deeper into the
Khazana of Khana, and come up
with what is best
and most precious in cuisine.

Acknowledgements

A.I. Kazi
Afsheen Panjwani
Anand Bhandiwad
Mrs. Lata Lohana & Capt. K. K. Lohana
Debashish Mukherjee
Dhiraj Bolur
Drs. Meena & Ram Prabhoo
Ganesh Pednekar
Harpal Singh Sokhi
Jijesh Gangadharan
Jyotsna & Mayur Dvivedi
Kishore Roy
Mallika Shetty
Manish Anand
Namita Pusalkar
Namrata & Sanjiv Bahl

Neelima Acharya
Neena Murdeshwar
Pallavi Sharma
Pooja & Rajeev Kapoor
Priti Surve
Rajeev Matta
Rutika Samtani
Sanjay Bakshi
Satish Parab
Shivani Ganesh
Smeeta Bhatkal
Swapna Shinde
Tripta Bhagattjee
Vinayak Gawande

Note to the Readers

It is heartening to see that the two ingredients of good food are easy to come by for those who love to eat and love to cook. The two ingredients are imagination and variety and it has been always my endeavour to bring forth books such as these that cater to all popular tastes. This collection, the second in the series of two books on snacks and starters, not only carries the everyday *kachoris* and *chaklis* but also a plethora of fresh ideas for you who love to dish up something new, something different and something worth trying out.

One ingredient that features greatly in many homes is *paneer*. *Paneer* is extremely versatile and once one is convinced that it is good for the family's health, then there is no limit to the number of dishes one can make with it. Here we have some snacks like *Paneer Koliwada* and *Crunchy Paneer Pakora* that prove that variety is the spice of life.

The traditional greats like *vadas* and *kachoris* are present in this collection for all those who want to avoid buying them from outside. Nothing like homemade, hygienic stuff! So do try your hand at the *Medu Wada* and *Urad Dal Ki Kachori*. Something that goes well with people who have the doctor's orders to have less oil is the *Dhokla* and the *Bombay Veg Sandwich*. Make the *Potato Chakli* in those adventurous moments and be ready to share the recipe once your friends taste it.

For those who love international cookery leaf through Mexican small bites like *Nachos*, and Chinese *Crispy Wontons* and the Middle Eastern filling snack of *Red Coleslaw in Pita Pockets*. The last is not only a healthy snack but also, thankfully, is attractive to a lot of fussy eaters as most children are. There are certain snacks that bear a familiar name but are very different looks wise. The best part is that these dishes with a difference have tremendous universal appeal. Here I am talking about the *Chilli Cheese Toast, Eggplant Pizza* (which I am sure will convert eggplant haters!) and the multi-hued, extremely attractive *Four Seasons Pizza*.

My efforts here are to convey that snacks can be healthy when made with healthful ingredients. If there is a fear that deep fried foods can harm you, go along that but remember that by sincerely working out, our metabolism can be altered to such efficiency that one can enjoy the eternal favourites! A happy palate brings forth a happy disposition and then the cup of happiness brims over. This goldmine awaits your attention and lest one forgets, all recipes serve four and form part of a menu.

CONTENTS

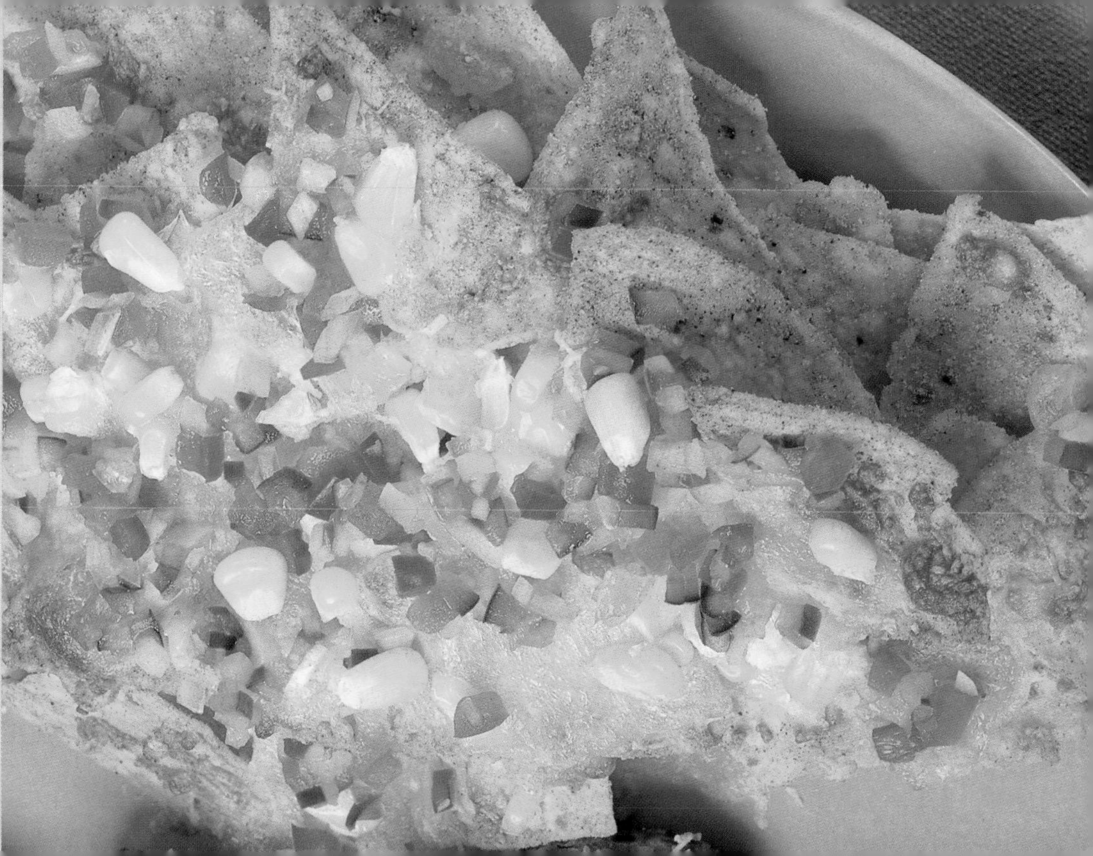

Nachos

NACHOS

INGREDIENTS

Tortilla or corn chips 16-20
Processed cheese (grated) ..... ¾ cup
For the salsa sauce
Tomatoes .... 2 large sized
Onion .... 1 medium sized
Garlic .... 2-3 cloves
Capsicum .... 1 medium sized
Peppercorns 5-6
Dry oregano .... ¼ tsp
Sweet chilli sauce .... 2 tbsps
Salt .... to taste

METHOD OF PREPARATION

1 Wash, halve, deseed and chop tomatoes. Peel, wash and chop onion. Peel, wash and crush garlic. Wash, halve, deseed and chop capsicum. Crush peppercorns.
2 Combine these with the rest of the ingredients and let this salsa sauce stand at room temperature for an hour before use.
3 Arrange corn chips on a baking tray, top it up with salsa sauce and grated cheese. Cook in the Grill (TOP) for two minutes.
4 Serve immediately otherwise the tortillas will turn soggy.

MEDU VADA

INGREDIENTS

Black gram split (*dhuli urad dal*). .... 1 cup
Salt .... to taste
Asafoetida .... ¼ tsp

Curry leaves 8-10
Cumin powder .... 1 tsp
Peppercorns (crushed) .... 1 tsp
Oil .... to deep fry

METHOD OF PREPARATION

1 Wash *dhuli urad dal* and soak in two cups of water for six hours. Drain and grind *dal* into a fine paste. Wash, pat dry and chop curry leaves.
2 Add salt, asafoetida, curry leaves, cumin powder and crushed peppercorns to the batter and mix well.
3 Heat sufficient oil in a *kadai*.
4 Wet your palms and take a little batter into your palms. Shape into balls and make a hole with the thumb in the center like a doughnut.
5 Deep fry in medium hot oil until golden brown and crisp. Drain onto an absorbent paper.
6 Serve hot with *sambhar* and coconut *chutney*.

PANEER KOLIWADA

INGREDIENTS

Cottage cheese (*paneer*) .. 300 gms
Gram flour (*besan*) .... ½ cup
Ginger .... 1 inch piece
Garlic .... 5-6 cloves
Cumin powder .... ½ tsp
Yogurt .... 2 tbsps

Kashmiri red chilli powder ... 2 tsps
Salt .... to taste
Lemon juice .... 2 tbsps
Oil .... to deep-fry
Chaat masala .... ½ tsp

METHOD OF PREPARATION

1 Cut *paneer* into finger sized pieces three inches x five inches x five inches.
2 Peel, wash and grind ginger and garlic to a paste.
3 Mix *besan*, cumin powder, yogurt, red chilli powder, salt, ginger-garlic paste and lemon juice. Add sufficient water to make a smooth thick batter.
4 Marinate *paneer* in this batter for half an hour.
5 Heat sufficient oil in a *kadai* and deep-fry *paneer* pieces till crisp on the outside.
6 Serve hot sprinkled with *chaat masala*.

DHOKLA

INGREDIENTS

Rice .... 1 cup
Black gram split (*dhuli urad dal*).
.... ¼ cup
Yogurt (sour) .... ¼ cup
Salt.................................... to taste
Green chillies 4

Ginger .... 1 inch piece
Fresh coriander leaves ... a few sprigs
Soda bicarbonate .... ½ tsp
Oil .... 2 tbsps
Lemon juice .... 1 tsp

METHOD OF PREPARATION

1   Dry roast rice and *dal* on medium heat for four to five minutes. Cool and grind into a semi-coarse powder.
2   Place powder in a bowl. Add yogurt and one and a half cups of warm water. Mix thoroughly so that no lumps are formed and the batter is of pouring consistency. Add salt and let it ferment for eight to ten hours.
3   Remove stems and wash green chillies. Peel, wash ginger and grind it with green chillies to a fine paste. Clean, wash and finely chop coriander leaves.

4 Once the batter is fermented, mix in the ginger-green chilli paste.

5 Grease the *dhokla* platter or a *thali*. Boil water in the steamer/boiler.

6 Pour half of the batter in another vessel. In a small bowl, add one-fourth teaspoon of soda bicarbonate, half a teaspoon of oil and half a teaspoon of lemon juice. Add this to the batter and mix well. Repeat this for the remaining batter just before putting it in the steamer.

7 Pour this onto the greased platter and steam it in the steamer for eight to ten minutes.

8 Check by inserting a knife. If the knife comes out clean, it is cooked.

9 Sprinkle finely chopped coriander leaves and serve hot with green *chutney*.

> **CHEF'S TIP**
>
> You can also put crushed peppercorns or red chilli powder over the *dhokla*. It is best enjoyed with *ghee*.

VEGETABLE CLUB SANDWICH

INGREDIENTS

Bread	12 slices	Pineapple slices	2
Carrot	1 medium sized	Mayonnaise sauce	¼ cup
Capsicum	1 medium sized	Salt	to taste
Cabbage	¼ medium sized	White pepper powder	¼ tsp
Lettuce	½ bunch	Butter	4 tbsps
Tomatoes	2 medium sized	Cheese slices	4
Cucumber	1 medium sized		

METHOD OF PREPARATION

1 Toast the bread slices. Peel, wash and grate carrot. Wash, halve, deseed and cut capsicum into thin strips. Wash, trim, remove core and grate cabbage. Trim, clean and wash lettuce. Pat dry.

2 Wash and cut tomatoes into slices. Peel, wash and cut cucumber into slices. Cut pineapple into small pieces.

3   Mix mayonnaise with capsicum, carrot and cabbage to make coleslaw. Add pineapple pieces to it. Season well.

4   Apply butter on all toasted bread slices on one side and on both the sides of four of them. Place four slices of bread, single side buttered, on a board. Arrange half of the lettuce leaves on them, keep some coleslaw aside for serving as accompaniment and spread the remaining evenly on all the four slices. Arrange another layer of bread slices, both sides buttered, on it. On this bread slice place remaining lettuce leaves, tomato and cucumber slices, sprinkle seasoning and place cheese slices.

5   Cover with the final layer of toasted bread slices, single side buttered. Lightly press with palm to set the ingredients well.

6   Using a very sharp knife cut the edges of the sandwich and cut it diagonally. Serve with coleslaw and potato wafers.

KAANDA POHA

INGREDIENTS

Thick *poha* .... 2 cups
Onions .... 3 medium sized
Green chillies 3-4
Fresh coriander leaves .... a few sprigs
Curry leaves 8-10

Roasted peanuts (optional) .. ¼ cup
Oil .... 2 tbsps
Turmeric powder .... 1 tsp
Salt .... to taste
Lemon juice .... 1 tbsp

METHOD OF PREPARATION

1 Wash *poha* thoroughly. Keep in a strainer so that excess water gets drained out.
2 Peel, wash and finely chop onions. Remove stems, wash, deseed and slit green chillies into two. Clean, wash and chop coriander leaves finely. Wash and pat dry curry leaves. Crush peanuts coarsely.
3 Heat oil in a pan. Add onions and stir fry on medium heat till they start turning brown. Add green chillies, curry leaves, crushed peanuts and continue to cook for two to three minutes.
4 Add turmeric powder, *poha* and salt. Mix well and cook, covered, on low heat for four to five minutes.
5 Add lemon juice. Mix well, garnish with chopped coriander leaves and serve hot.

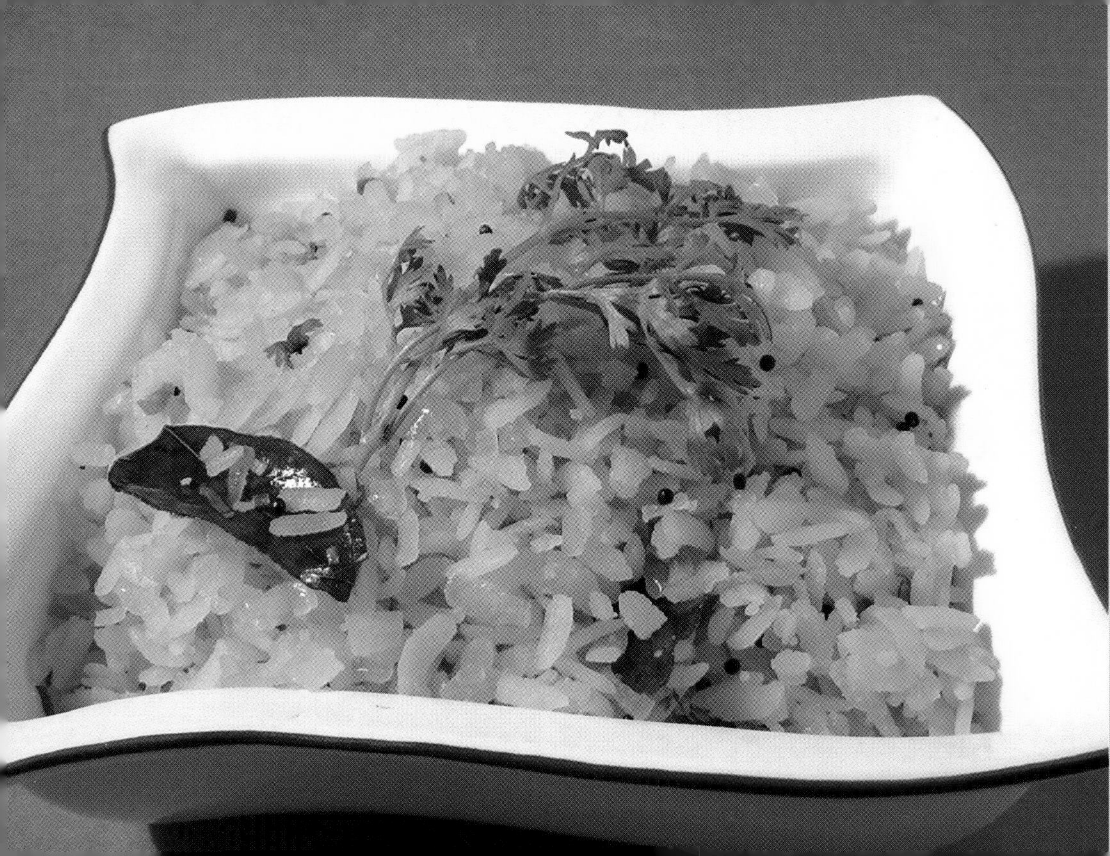

Kaanda Poha

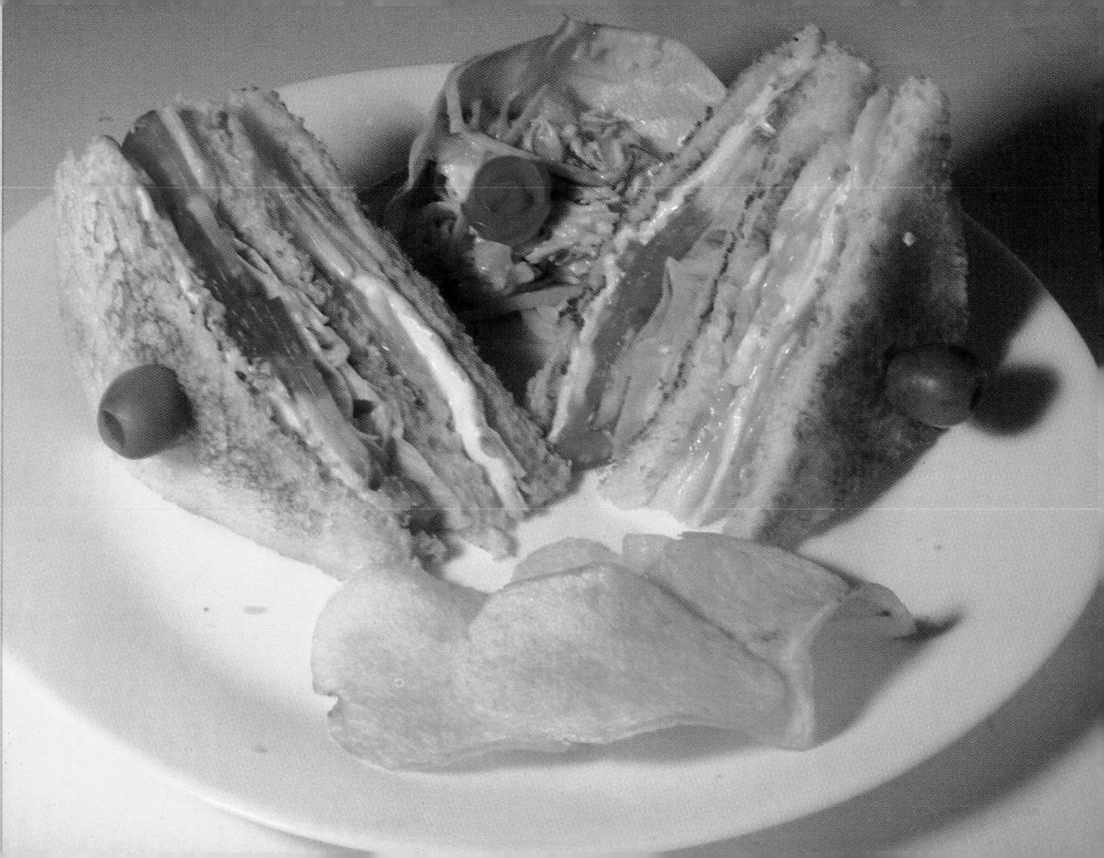

Vegetable Club Sandwich

Khasta Kachori

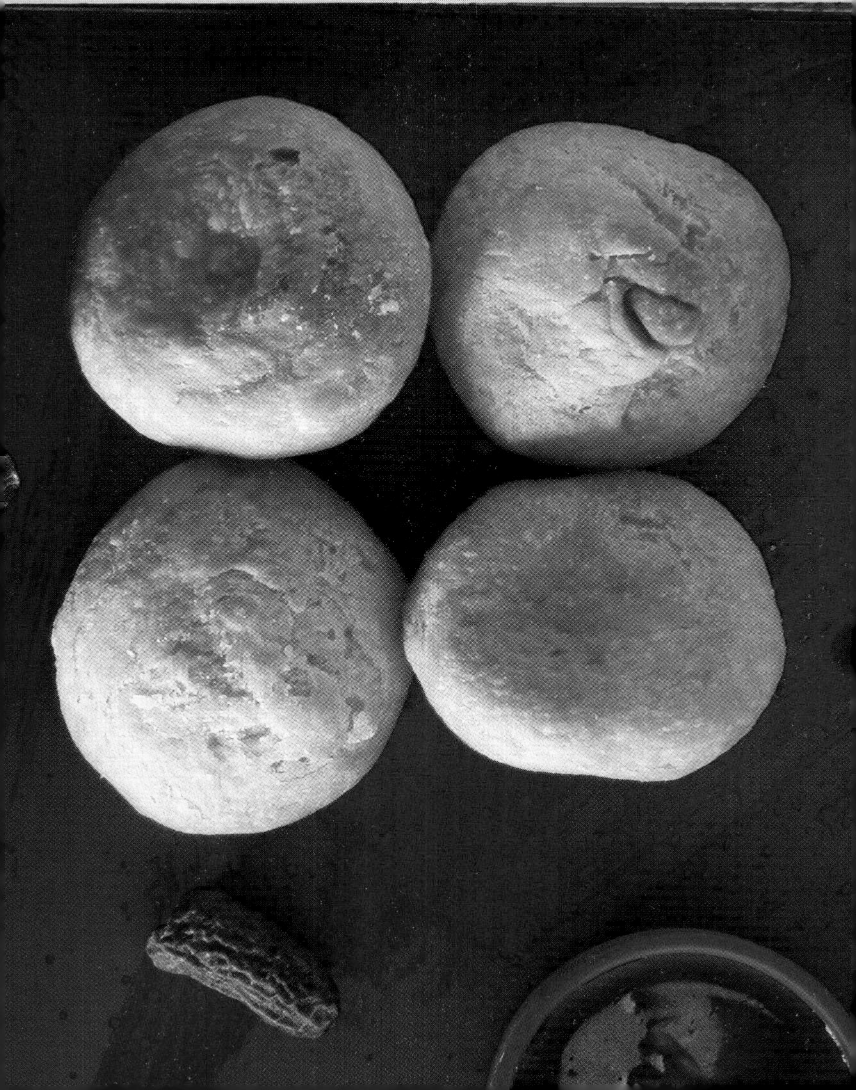

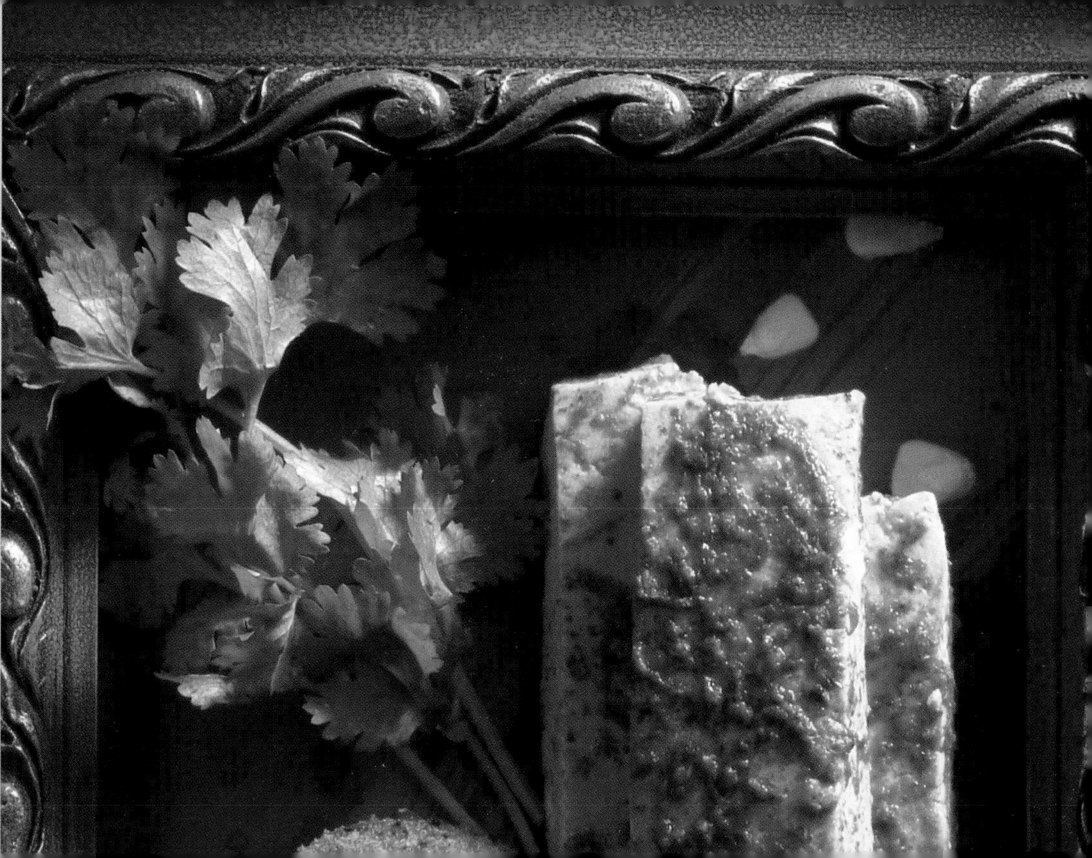

Hariyali Paneer

HARIYALI PANEER

INGREDIENTS

Cottage cheese (*paneer*) .... 500 gms
Oil .... 1 tbsp + to shallow fry
Butter (optional) .... to baste
Green *masala*
Fresh coriander leaves ....
.... a small bunch
Green chillies 2-3
Ginger .... 1 inch piece

Raw mango .... 1 small sized
Gram flour (*besan*) .... 2 tbsps
Cumin seeds .... ½ tsp
Peppercorns 6
Cloves 6
Cinnamon powder .... 1 tbsp
Rock salt (*sendha namak*) .... to taste
Chaat masala .... 2 tsps

METHOD OF PREPARATION

1   Cut *paneer* into one-inch sized cubes.
2   Clean, wash and chop coriander leaves. Remove stems, wash and roughly chop green chillies. Wash, peel and chop ginger. Peel, wash, deseed and chop raw mango.

3   Dry roast gram flour in a pan till it gives out a nice aroma.
4   Grind together coriander leaves, green chillies, ginger, raw mango, cumin seeds, peppercorns, cloves and cinnamon powder to a fine paste adding a little water if required. Add *sendha namak* and mix well. Add roasted gram flour and one tablespoon of oil. Mix well.
5   Coat *paneer* pieces with this paste and keep aside for fifteen minutes.
6   Heat sufficient oil in a *kadai* and shallow fry *paneer* pieces till they turn light brown on both sides.
7   Drain onto an absorbent paper. Sprinkle with *chaat masala* and serve hot.
8   Alternatively you can cook *paneer* pieces in a preheated oven at 250°C for twenty minutes frequently basting with butter.

KHASTA KACHORI

INGREDIENTS

Refined flour (*maida*) .... 2 cups
Salt.................................... to taste
Soda bicarbonate .... ½ tsp
Oil.................................... 5 tbsps
For filling
Black gram split (*dhuli urad dal*).
.... ½ cup
Ginger .... 1 inch piece
Green chilli 1
Cashewnuts 6-8
Raisins 10-12

Ghee .... 3 tbsps
Asafoetida .... a pinch
Coriander powder .... 1 tsp
Cumin powder.................... ½ tsp
Red chilli powder .... 1 tsp
Fennel (*saunf*) powder .... ¼ tsp
Sugar .... ½ tsp
Salt .... to taste
Lemon juice .... 1 tbsp
Oil .... to deep fry

METHOD OF PREPARATION

1 Sift flour, salt and soda bicarbonate together. Add oil and mix well. Knead into a soft dough using sufficient water. Cover with a moist cloth and set aside.

2 Wash *urad dal* well and soak in two cups of water for an hour. Drain and coarsely grind using a little water.

3 Peel, wash and finely chop ginger. Remove stem, wash and chop green chilli. Roughly chop cashewnuts. Wash raisins and pat dry.

4 Heat *ghee* in a *kadai* and add ground *dal*, ginger, green chilli, asafoetida, coriander powder, cumin powder, red chilli powder, fennel powder, cashewnuts and raisins. Cook till all the moisture has dried up.

5 Add sugar, salt and lemon juice. Mix well and remove from heat and let mixture cool. Divide into sixteen portions.

6 Divide flour dough into sixteen equal balls. Roll out into small *puris* so that they are thinner around the edges and thicker in the centre.

7 Place a portion of stuffing in the centre and bring edges together to form a ball. Flatten slightly.

8 Heat sufficient oil in a *kadai* and deep fry *kachoris* on low heat for three to five minutes or until golden brown and crisp.

9 Serve with tamarind *chutney*.

PIQUANT POTATOES IN JACKETS

INGREDIENTS

Potatoes	4 large sized	Cumin seeds	1 tsp
Onion	1 small sized	Turmeric powder	½ tsp
Ginger	1 inch piece	Coriander powder	2 tsps
Garlic	3-4 cloves	Pepper powder	½ tsp
Fresh coriander leaves	a few sprigs	Garlic salt	1 tsp
Oil	1 tbsp	Yogurt	8 tbsps

METHOD OF PREPARATION

1 Wash and prick potatoes with a fork. Preheat oven to 190°C.
2 Bake in a preheated oven at 190°C for forty minutes or till done.
3 Cut potatoes in half and scoop out flesh without spoiling the skin. Skin of the potato is popularly known as the jacket.
4 Peel, wash and finely chop onion. Peel, wash and finely chop ginger and garlic. Clean, wash and chop coriander leaves.

5 Heat oil in a pan. Add cumin seeds, onion, ginger and garlic. Sauté for a minute.
6 Add scooped potatoes, turmeric powder, coriander powder, pepper powder and garlic salt.
7 Cook further on medium heat for two minutes, stirring occasionally. Adjust seasoning.
8 Spoon mixture back into potato jackets and top each with a tablespoonful of yogurt.
9 Garnish with chopped coriander leaves and serve hot.

URAD DAL KI KACHORI

INGREDIENTS

Black gram split (*dhuli urad dal*). .... 1 cup
Refined flour (*maida*) .... 3 cups
Green chillies 2
Ginger .... 1 inch piece
Fresh coriander leaves ... a few sprigs

Cumin seeds .... 1 tsp
Oil .... 4 tbsps + to deep-fry
Asafoetida .... a pinch
Chaat masala .... 1 tsp
Salt .... to taste

METHOD OF PREPARATION

1   Wash *dhuli urad dal* well and soak in three cups of water for three to four hours. Drain and grind coarsely.
2   Remove stems, wash and finely chop green chillies. Peel, wash and finely chop ginger. Clean, wash and chop coriander leaves. Coarsely powder cumin seeds.

3   Take two tablespoons of oil in a frying pan, add asafoetida, green
    chillies, ginger, coriander leaves, *chaat masala* and coarsely ground
    cumin seeds. Mix well and add salt to taste. Add ground *dal*. Mix
    and continue to sauté for two to three minutes till mixture is dry.
    Remove from heat and divide into twelve to sixteen portions.

4   Sieve *maida* and mix in two tablespoons of oil and salt to taste.
    Knead into a stiff dough using water as required.

5   Divide dough into twelve to sixteen portions and roll into small
    balls. Flatten slightly and stuff a portion of the *dal* mixture. Shape
    into a ball and roll into three-inch *puris* so that they are thinner
    around the edges and thicker in the center.

6   Heat sufficient oil in a *kadai*. When moderately hot, add a few
    kachoris. Continue to fry on low heat, turning *kachoris* once to twice
    till crisp and golden. Drain onto an absorbent kitchen paper.

7   Serve hot with any pickle, *chutney* or sauce of your choice.

MUSHROOM AND PANEER KABAB

INGREDIENTS

Fresh button mushrooms 14-16
Cottage cheese (*paneer*) .. 200 gms
Onions ....3 medium sized
Capsicums .... 2 large sized
Cherry tomatoes 18-20
Green chillies 2-3
Ginger .... 2 inch piece
Garlic .... 8-10 cloves

Oil .... 2 tsps
Red chilli flakes .... 1 tsps
Honey .... 2 tsps
Cumin powder .... 1 tsp
Garam masala powder .... 1 tsp
Salt .... to taste
Lemon juice .... 2 tsps
Chaat masala .... 1 tsp

METHOD OF PREPARATION

1 Clean and wash mushrooms. Cut *paneer* into one and half inch sized cubes. Peel, wash and cut onions into one-inch sized chunks. Wash, halve, deseed and cut capsicums into one-inch sized pieces. Wash cherry tomatoes.

2   Remove stems, wash, deseed and roughly chop green chillies. Peel, wash ginger and garlic and grind to a paste along with green chillies.

3   In a bowl mix together oil, ginger-garlic-green chilli paste, red chilli flakes, honey, cumin powder, *garam masala* powder, salt, lemon juice and *chaat masala*.

4   Marinate *paneer*, button mushrooms, cherry tomatoes, capsicum and onion chunks in this mixture for about an hour.

5   Take eight-inch long wooden satay sticks or skewers and soak them in water for half an hour. Remove from water and thread marinated *paneer* cubes, mushrooms, cherry tomatoes, capsicum and onion pieces one after the other on the sticks or skewers.

6   Cook on an open charcoal fire or directly over gas flame for five minutes, rotating the stick for even cooking. Alternatively, cook in a preheated oven at 180° C for about fifteen minutes.

CHILLI TACOS

INGREDIENTS

Taco shells 8

Lettuce (preferably iceberg) ....
.... ½ bunch

Spring onions 2

Green chillies 2

Fresh mint leaves ...... a few sprigs

Cherry tomatoes 8

Low fat cheese (grated) ... ½ cup

Cheddar cheese (grated) ... ½ cup

Baked beans in tomato sauce .....
.... 1 cup

Chilli sauce .... 2 tsps

Lemon juice .... 2 tbsps

Salt .... to taste

Pepper powder .... ½ tsp

METHOD OF PREPARATION

1   Wash lettuce well under running water and shred. Trim, wash and chop spring onions. Remove stems, wash, slit into two, deseed and finely chop green chillies. Clean, wash and chop half of the mint leaves keeping aside the rest for garnish.

2   Wash and quarter cherry tomatoes. Preheat oven to 180°C.
3   Warm the taco shells in a preheated oven at 180°C for three to four minutes.
4   In a bowl take baked beans and add grated low fat cheese, onions, chilli sauce, lemon juice and chopped mint leaves. Add salt and pepper powder, mix lightly.
5   Fill taco shells till about three-fourths full with shredded lettuce and spoon baked beans mixture on top of the shredded lettuce leaves evenly.
6   Top shells with grated Cheddar cheese, quartered cherry tomatoes and a sprig of mint.
7   Serve immediately.

CHEF'S TIP

Though the taco shells are fried, since the quantity of salad used is more it becomes a healthy meal with controlled calories.

THREE FLAVOUR POPCORN

Sweet

INGREDIENTS

Dried corn kernels .... ½ cup   Oil .... 1 tbsp
Brown sugar .... ¾ cup

METHOD OF PREPARATION

Mix oil, brown sugar and corn in a bowl. Preheat a pressure cooker without gasket for two to three minutes on medium heat. Transfer corn into it and put lid into place. Place on high heat and shake cooker once the popping of popcorn begins. Remove from heat after two to three minutes or when the popping sounds stop coming. Open and serve warm.

Savoury

INGREDIENTS

Dried corn kernels .... ½ cup	Cheese powder .... 2 tbsps
Oil .... 1 tbsp	Red chilli flakes .... 1½ tbsps

METHOD OF PREPARATION

Mix oil and corn in a bowl. Preheat a pressure cooker without gasket for two to three minutes on medium heat. Transfer corn into it and put lid into place. Place on high heat and shake cooker once the popping of popcorn begins. Remove from heat after two to three minutes or when the popping sounds stop coming. Open, add cheese powder and red chilli flakes and toss. Serve immediately.

Savoury

INGREDIENTS

Dried corn kernels .... ½ cup	Tomato powder .... 1 tbsp
Oil .... 1 tbsp	Salt .... to taste

METHOD OF PREPARATION

Mix oil and corn in a bowl. Preheat a pressure cooker without gasket for two to three minutes on medium heat. Transfer corn into it and put lid into place. Place on high heat and shake cooker once the popping of popcorn begins. Remove from heat after two to three minutes or when the popping sounds stop coming. Open, add tomato powder and salt to taste and toss. Serve immediately.

CHEF'S TIP

Try out an interesting combination of all the popcorns namely caramel, chilli cheese and tomato. It happened to me once accidentally!

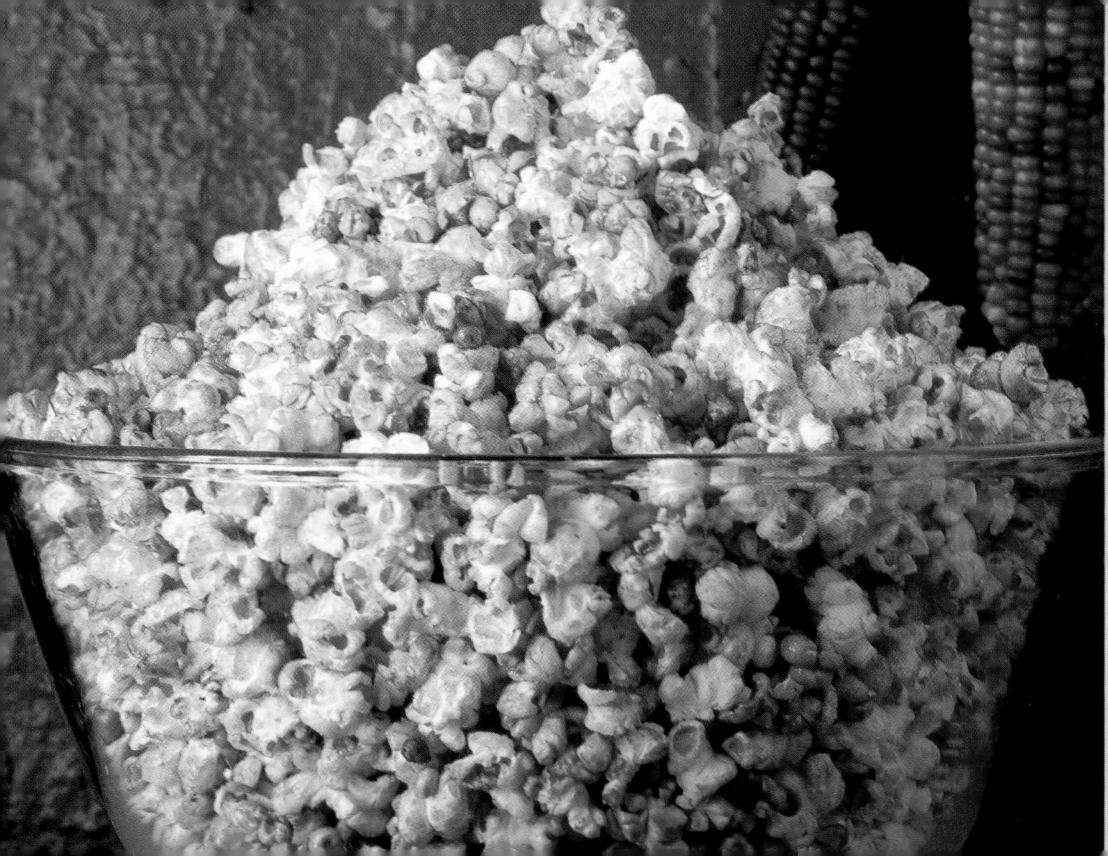

Three Flavour Popcorn

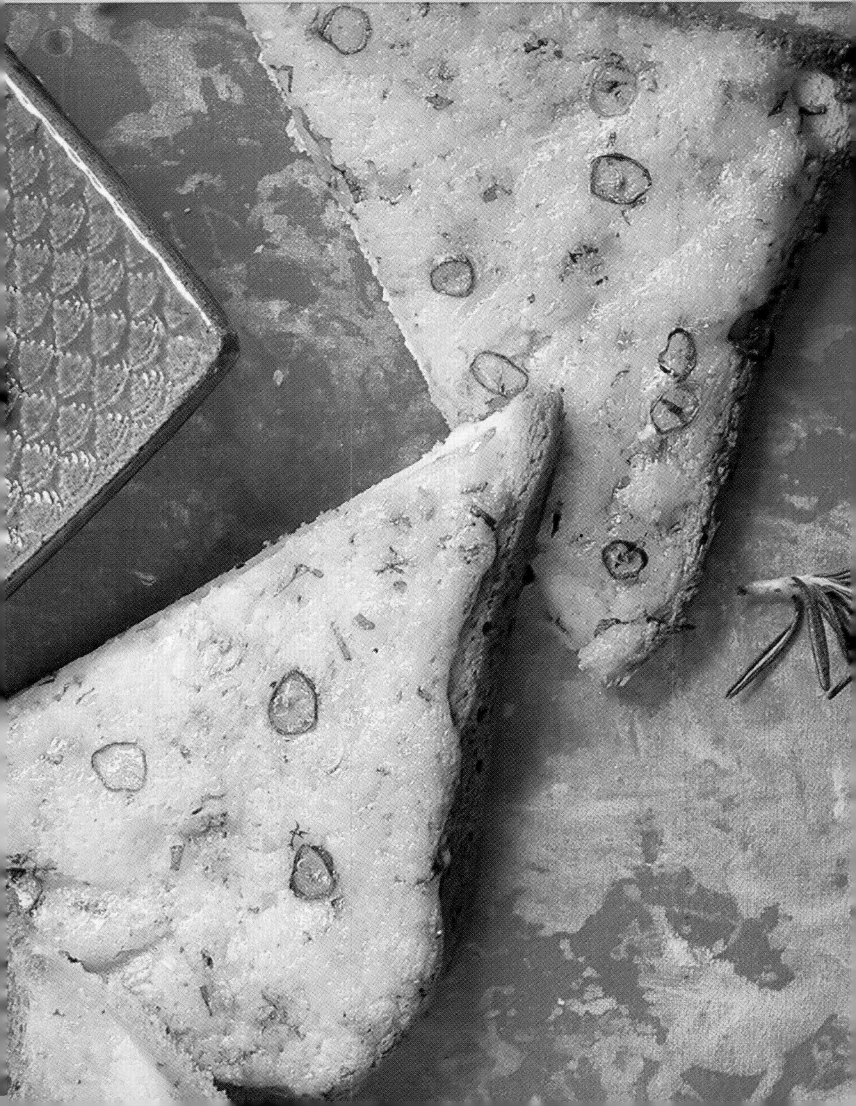

Chilli Cheese Toast

CHILLI CHEESE TOAST

INGREDIENTS

Bread .... 8 slices
Cheese (grated) .... 1½ cups
Green chillies 4-6
Fresh coriander leaves ....
.... ½ medium bunch

Onion ....: 1 medium sized
Capsicum (optional) ....
.... 1 medium sized
Peppercorns (crushed) .... 1 tsp
Salt .... to taste

METHOD OF PREPARATION

1 Remove stems, wash and finely chop green chillies. Clean, wash and chop coriander leaves. Peel, wash and chop onion. Wash, halve, deseed and chop capsicum.

2 In a bowl, mix cheese, green chillies, coriander leaves, onion, capsicum, crushed peppercorns and salt. Divide the mixture into eight equal portions.

3 Toast bread slices on one side on a *tawa*.

4 Apply cheese mixture on non-toasted side of bread slices. Preheat oven to 180° C.

5 Grill in a preheated oven (180° C) till cheese melts and turns golden brown.

6 Cut each slice diagonally into two and serve hot with a sauce of your choice.

PARUPPU WADA

INGREDIENTS

Pigeon pea split (*toovar dal*) ... ½ cup
Bengal gram split (*chana dal*) .....
.... ½ cup
Black gram split (*dhuli urad dal*).
.... ½ cup
Onion .... 1 large sized
Ginger .... ½ inch piece
Green chillies 4

Curry leaves 10-12
Fresh coriander leaves ....
.... ¼ small bunch
Red chillies whole 4
Salt .... to taste
Asafoetida .... ¼ tsp
Oil .... to deep fry

METHOD OF PREPARATION

1   Wash and soak all the *dals* together in three cups of water for half
    an hour. Drain the water completely by keeping in a colander.
2   Peel, wash and chop onion and ginger. Remove stems, wash and
    chop green chillies. Wash and pat dry curry leaves. Clean, wash
    and chop coriander leaves. Remove stems of red chillies.

3 Grind soaked *dals* coarsely with red chillies, curry leaves, ginger and salt using a little water if required.

4 Transfer the batter into a bowl, add onion, green chillies, asafoetida, coriander leaves and mix well. Adjust salt.

5 Heat sufficient oil in a *kadai*. Shape batter into one and a half-inch diameter balls, press slightly and deep fry over medium heat till golden brown and crisp.

6 Drain onto an absorbent paper and serve hot with any *chutney* of your choice.

POTATO SKINS

INGREDIENT

Potatoes .... 4 large sized	Peppercorns (crushed) .... ½ tsp
Oil .... to deep-fry	Fresh cream .... 2 tbsps
Cheese (grated) .... 2 tbsps	Lemon juice .... 1 tsp
Onion .... 1 small sized	Salt .... to taste
Fresh coriander leaves ... a few sprigs	

METHOD OF PREPARATION

1. Wash potatoes and parboil in five cups of water. Cut into long pieces. Remove pulp with a spoon leaving a little pulp on the skin.
2. Heat sufficient oil in a *kadai*, deep fry potato pieces in hot oil. Drain and keep on an absorbent paper.
3. Peel, wash and finely chop onion. Clean, wash and finely chop fresh coriander leaves.
4. Beat fresh cream and add lemon juice to it.
5. In bowl, take grated cheese. Add onion, coriander leaves, beaten cream, crushed peppercorns and salt.
6. Put this topping on fried potato skins and serve hot.

SOYA SHAMMI KABAB

INGREDIENTS

Soya *wadi* .... 1 ¼ cups
Bengal gram split *(chana dal)* ...
.... ½ cup
Ginger .... 1 inch piece
Garlic .... 5 cloves
Green chillies 2
Red chillies whole 4
Cloves 4

Cinnamon .... 1 inch stick
Bay leaf 1
Dry pomegranate seeds *(anardana)*
.... 1 tsp
Oil .... 1 tbsp + to deep-fry
Salt .... to taste
Breadcrumbs .... 1 cup

METHOD OF PREPARATION

1 Soak soya *wadi* in hot water for about twenty minutes. Squeeze out excess water.

2 Pick and wash *chana dal*. Peel, wash and grate ginger. Peel, wash

and chop garlic. Remove stems, wash and chop green chillies. Remove stems and break red chillies into two.

3   Tie cloves, cinnamon and bay leaf in a piece of cloth to make a small *potli*. Finely crush *anardana* and keep aside.

4   Heat one tablespoon of oil in a pan, add the *potli* and stir-fry for about two minutes. Add ginger, garlic, red chillies and green chillies and continue to cook for another couple of minutes.

5   Add soya *wadi* and *chana dal*, stir for five minutes. Add a cup of water, mix well and then lower heat. Cook until *dal* is cooked and liquid dries completely.

6   Cool mixture thoroughly, discard *potli*, and grind mixture to a fine paste.

7   Add *anardana*, salt and bread crumbs and knead into a stiff dough.

8   Divide into equal portions. Shape each portion into a round *tikki* shape.

9   Heat sufficient oil in a *kadai*. Deep-fry *tikkis* in moderately hot oil until golden brown and crisp. Drain onto an absorbent paper.

10 Serve immediately with any spicy sauce.

MOONG KE CHEELAY

INGREDIENTS

Green gram split (*moong dal*) ...
.... 1 cup
Cumin seeds......................... 1 tsp
Green chillies 2
Asafoetida .... a pinch
Salt.................................. to taste

Onion .... 1 medium sized
Tomato .... 1 medium sized
Fresh coriander leaves ... a few sprigs
Cottage cheese (*paneer*) ... 100 gms
Red chilli powder .... ½ tsp
Oil .... to shallow fry

METHOD OF PREPARATION

1   Pick, clean and wash *moong dal*. Soak in two cups of water for two hours. Remove stems, wash and roughly chop green chillies. Grind *moong dal* with cumin seeds and green chillies. Dissolve asafoetida in two tablespoons of water and mix it into the *dal* batter. Add salt and mix well.

2   Peel, wash and chop onion. Wash and chop tomato. Clean, wash and chop coriander leaves. Grate *paneer* and mix onion, tomato and coriander leaves. Season with salt and red chilli powder. Keep aside.

3   Heat oil on a *tawa* or in a frying pan. Spoon a ladle full of batter onto the *tawa* and spread it to make a pancake with a diameter of about four to five inches. Shallow fry for about half a minute.

4   Sprinkle about two tablespoons of *paneer* topping over the *cheelah*. Spoon a little oil on the sides of the *cheelah* and cook for fifteen seconds on medium heat.

5   Turn the *cheelah* over and let it cook on the other side for two minutes on low to medium heat. Spoon oil on the sides of the *cheelah* and turn it over. Cook for another minute on moderately high heat. Serve hot with *chutney* of your choice.

Bhutte Ke Cutlet

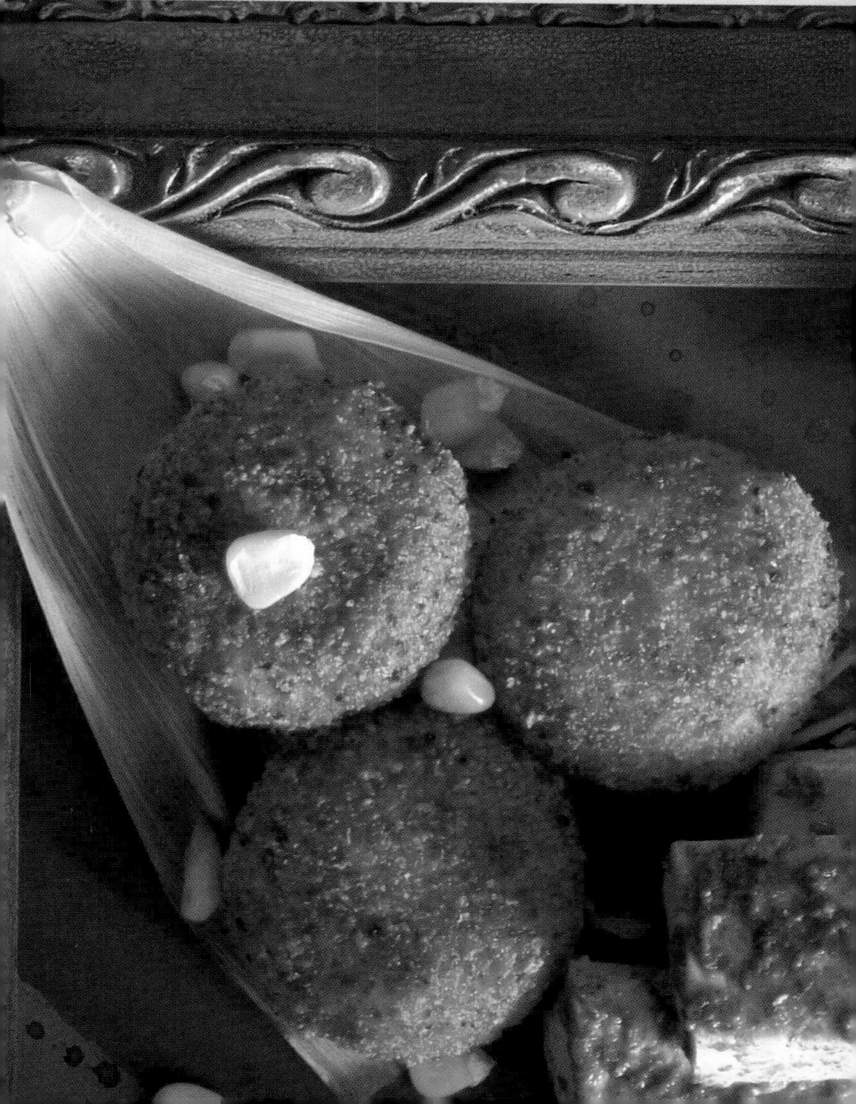

BHUTTE KE CUTLET

INGREDIENTS

Corn niblets .... 1 cup	Fennel (*saunf*) seeds .... 1 tsp
Onions .... 2 medium sized	Turmeric powder .... ½ tsp
Green chillies 4-6	Coriander powder .... 1 tsp
Ginger .... 2 inch piece	Red chilli powder .... 1 tsp
Fresh coriander leaves	*Garam masala* powder .... 1 tsp
.... 1 medium bunch	Salt .... to taste
Gram flour (*besan*) .... ¼ cup	Breadcrumbs .... ¼ cup
Oil .... 2 tbsps + to deep-fry	Lemon juice .... 2 tbsps
Cumin seeds .... 1 tsp	*Chaat masala* .... 2 tbsps

METHOD OF PREPARATION

1　Boil corn niblets or pressure cook them in two cups of water and cool. Squeeze them in a muslin cloth to drain excess water.

2   Peel, wash and chop onions. Remove stems, wash and chop green chillies. Peel, wash and chop ginger. Clean, wash and chop coriander leaves. Roast gram flour in a pan till it gives a nice aroma.

3   Heat two tablespoons of oil in a pan, add cumin seeds and fennel seeds and sauté till they change colour. Add onions and sauté till light brown in colour.

4   Add turmeric powder, coriander powder, red chilli powder and *garam masala* powder. Stir to mix well. Add half of the cooked corn niblets and sauté till dry. Remove from heat, cool slightly and grind in a mixer. Remove into a bowl.

5   Add the rest of the cooked corn niblets, coriander leaves and salt to taste.

6   Add gram flour, breadcrumbs and mix well to form a dough. Make sixteen equal cutlets.

7   Heat sufficient oil in a *kadai* and deep fry cutlets till golden brown in colour. Drain onto an absorbent kitchen towel.

8   Sprinkle lemon juice and *chaat masala* and serve hot.

CHATPATI TIKKI

INGREDIENTS

Raw bananas ...... 2 medium sized
Carrots .... 2 medium sized
Onion .... 1 medium sized
Ginger .... 1 inch piece
Green chillies 3-4
Fresh mint leaves 8-10
Raisins 15-20
Dates (seedless) 6
Roasted peanuts (without skin) ......
.... ½ cup

Oil .... 1 tsp
Mustard seeds .... ½ tsp
Black gram split (*dhuli urad dal*)
.... ½ tsp
Red chilli powder .... 1 tsp
Chaat masala .... 2 tsps
Salt .... to taste
Lemon juice .... 2 tsps

METHOD OF PREPARATION

1 Boil whole raw bananas in two to three cups of water for fifteen to twenty minutes. Cool, peel and mash well. Peel, wash and grate carrots.
2 Peel, wash and finely chop onion and ginger. Remove stems, wash and finely chop green chillies. Wash and finely chop mint leaves.

3 Wash, pat dry and roughly chop raisins and seedless dates. Divide into twelve equal portions.
4 Grind roasted peanuts to a coarse powder. Keep aside.
5 Heat oil in a non-stick pan and add mustard seeds. As they begin to crackle and add *dhuli urad dal* and as it begins to brown, add onion, ginger and green chillies. Stir-fry for half a minute.
6 Add red chilli powder, mix and quickly add grated carrots.
7 Cook over medium heat for two to three minutes. Sprinkle mint leaves, *chaat masala*, mix well and remove from heat.
8 Cool and mix cooked *masala* with mashed raw bananas. Add salt to taste, lemon juice and mix well.
9 Divide mixture into twelve equal portions. Stuff a portion of dates-raisin mixture into each portion of raw banana mixture.
10 Wet your palm and form into patties (*tikkis*) of not more than half an inch thickness.
11 Coat the *tikkis* with coarse peanut powder, pressing them lightly with your palms.
12 Heat a non-stick frying pan or a griddle plate (*tawa*), place the peanut coated *tikkis*. Cook on medium heat till the crust is crisp and nicely browned. Make sure that the *tikkis* are heated through.
13 Serve immediately with a tangy sauce of your choice.

BOMBAY VEG SANDWICH

INGREDIENTS

Bread .... 8 slices
Onions .... 2 medium sized
Cucumber .... 1 large sized
Tomatoes .... 2 medium sized
Potatoes .... 2 medium sized

Butter .... 2 tbsps
Coriander & mint chutney ... ½ cup
Chaat masala .... ½ tsp
Salt .... to taste
Peppercorns (crushed) .... ½ tsp

METHOD OF PREPARATION

1   Peel, wash and cut onions and cucumber into roundels. Wash and cut tomatoes into roundels.
2   Wash and boil potatoes. Allow them to cool. Peel and slice.
3   Trim sides of bread slices, apply butter and coriander and mint *chutney*.
4   On a flat board, arrange four bread slices with chutney spread, layer it with onion, cucumber, tomato roundels and potato slices. Sprinkle some *chaat masala*, salt and crushed peppercorns. Cover each of them with another slice of bread and press lightly.
5   Cut each sandwich into six equal portions and serve with tomato ketchup.

PANEER WITH PESTO SAUCE

INGREDIENTS

Cottage cheese (*paneer*) .... 500 gms
Red chillies whole 4-5
Ginger .... 1 inch piece
Peppercorns 6
Cloves 6
Cinnamon powder .... 1 tbsp
Salt.................................... to taste
Lemon juice .... 2 tbsps

Oil .... to deep fry
Pesto sauce
Fresh basil leaves 10-12
Fresh parsley .... a few sprigs
Garlic............................. 5-6 cloves
Pinenuts (*chilgoza*) .... ¼ cup
Salt .... to taste
Olive oil .... 1 tbsp

METHOD OF PREPARATION

1 Cut *paneer* into thick slices.
2 Remove stems and break red chillies into two. Peel, wash and chop ginger.

3   Grind together red chillies, ginger, peppercorns, cloves and cinnamon powder to a fine paste. Add salt and lemon juice and mix well.

4   Coat *paneer* with the above paste and keep aside to marinate.

5   To make pesto sauce, wash and drain basil leaves and fresh parsley. Peel and wash garlic. Peel pinenuts. Blend these adding salt and olive oil to make a smooth sauce.

6   Heat sufficient oil in a *kadai* and deep-fry *paneer* pieces till lightly browned on both sides. Serve hot with pesto sauce.

RICE PAKORAS

INGREDIENTS

Rice (cooked) .... 2 cups
Gram flour (besan) ..... 4-5 tbsps
Onion .... 1 medium sized
Ginger .... 1 inch piece
Green chillies 2-3

Fresh coriander leaves ... a few sprigs
Chaat masala .... 1 tsp
Salt .... to taste
Oil .... to deep-fry

METHOD OF PREPARATION

1   Peel, wash and finely chop onion and ginger. Remove stems, wash and finely chop green chillies. Clean, wash and finely chop coriander leaves.
2   Mix cooked rice, besan, onion, ginger, green chillies, coriander leaves, chaat masala and salt to taste. Add about one-fourth cup of water to make a thick batter.
3   Heat sufficient oil in a kadai to moderate heat.
4   Spoon the batter with a tablespoon into hot oil and deep fry till light golden brown.
5   Drain onto an absorbent paper and fry once again in very hot oil briefly.
6   Serve hot with chutney of your choice.

Note : For this recipe you may also use leftover cooked rice.

EGG PLANT PIZZA

INGREDIENTS

Egg plants .... 2 large sized
Salt .... to taste
Garlic .... 10-12 cloves
Fresh basil leaves 6-7
Onion .... 1 medium sized
Fresh button mushrooms 2-3
Green capsicum ...... ½ large sized
Yellow capsicum ..... ½ large sized

Red capsicum .... ½ large sized
Refined flour (*maida*) .... ½ cup
Pepper powder .... ½ tsp
Olive oil .... 5 tbsps
Tomato concasse .... 1 cup
Peppercorns (crushed) ..... ½ tbsp
Processed cheese (grated) .... 1 cup

METHOD OF PREPARATION

1   Wash egg plants and cut them into one-centimeter thick roundels.
    Apply some salt and keep aside for ten to fifteen minutes.

2   Peel, wash and chop garlic. Clean, wash and pat dry fresh basil leaves.

3   Peel, wash and slice onion. Clean, wash and slice mushrooms. Wash
    green, yellow and red capsicums, deseed and cut into julienne. Mix
    all these together and keep aside.

4   Sieve refined flour with pepper powder and salt.

5   Wash egg plant slices and pat dry with a kitchen towel. Coat with seasoned flour.

6   Heat four tablespoons of olive oil in a pan and pan-fry eggplant slices on both sides till golden brown but still firm. Transfer them onto an absorbent paper and keep warm.

7   Heat one tablespoon of olive oil in another pan, add garlic and sauté. Add tomato concasse, salt, freshly crushed pepper and basil leaves. Stir and cook till dry.

8   Once the tomato sauce is ready, spread it on the fried egg plant pieces. Spread onion mixture and cover with grated cheese.

9   Place under a hot grill till cheese melts and turns golden. Serve immediately.

METHI BHAJIA

INGREDIENTS

Fresh fenugreek leaves (*methi*) ...
.... 2 medium bunches
Onion .... 1 medium sized
Oil .... 1 tbsp + to deep fry
Gram flour (*besan*) .... ½ cup
Red chilli powder .... 1 tsp

Salt .... to taste
Turmeric .... ½ tsp
Sugar .... 1 tsp
Carom seeds (*ajwain*) .... ¼ tsp
Soda bicarbonate .... a pinch

METHOD OF PREPARATION

1 Clean, wash and chop *methi* leaves. Peel, wash and finely chop onion.
2 Heat one tablespoon of oil in a *kadai*. Add *methi* and onion and sauté for two minutes. Add *besan* and other ingredients.
3 Add a little water to make a batter of dropping consistency.
4 Heat sufficient oil in a *kadai* and add a teaspoonful of the batter and deep fry in hot oil till crisp and golden.
5 Drain onto an absorbent paper and serve hot with *chutney* of your choice.

PHODNICHI BHAKRI

INGREDIENTS

Jowar/Bajri Bhakri 4

Peanuts .... ½ cup

Onion .... 1 medium sized

Green chillies 2

Fresh coriander leaves ... a few sprigs

Oil .... 1 tbsp

Mustard seeds .... ½ tsp

Salt .... to taste

Coconut (scraped) .... ¼ cup

METHOD OF PREPARATION

1 Crush the leftover *jowar* or *bajri bhakris*.
2 Roast peanuts. Cool and remove skin. Grind into a coarse powder.
3 Peel, wash and finely chop onion. Remove stems, wash and slit green chillies into two. Clean, wash and finely chop coriander leaves.
4 Heat oil in a pan. Add mustard seeds. When seeds begin to crackle, add onion and green chillies and sauté for a minute.
5 Add crushed *bhakri* and roasted peanut powder and season with salt.
6 Add coconut and coriander leaves and serve hot.

MIRCHI WADA

INGREDIENTS

Green chillies.......... 8 large sized
Potatoes .... 6-7 medium sized
Fresh coriander leaves ... a few sprigs
Red chilli powder .... 1 tbsp
Garam masala powder ...... 1 tbsp
Chaat masala .... 1 tsp
Salt................................. to taste

For batter
Gram flour *(besan)* .... 1 cup
Baking powder..................... 1 tsp
Red chilli powder .... 1 tsp
Salt .... to taste
Oil .... to deep fry

METHOD OF PREPARATION

1 Wash, wipe dry green chillies. Slit and remove seeds. Clean, wash
   and chop coriander leaves.
2 Wash, boil, cool, peel and grate potatoes. Add red chilli powder,
   garam masala powder, *chaat masala*, chopped coriander leaves and
   salt. Mix well. Divide into sixteen equal portions.
3 Stuff a little of this mixture into the green chillies and also cover
   the chillies with this potato mixture.

4   Prepare a thick batter using *besan*, baking powder, red chilli powder, salt and about one cup of water. Keep batter for ten minutes.

5   Heat sufficient oil in a *kadai* to a moderate temperature. Dip stuffed green chillies into *besan* batter and deep fry until golden brown. Remove, drain onto an absorbent kitchen paper and serve hot.

Note: Select large sized green chillies for this recipe. It will not only give it a nice definite shape but also would not be very hot.

KHAMAN DHOKLA

INGREDIENTS

Gram flour (*besan*) .... 2 cups
Yogurt .... 1 cup
Salt .... to taste
Green chillies 3
Ginger .... 1 inch piece
Fresh coriander leaves .... a few sprigs

Turmeric powder .... ½ tsp
Oil .... 2 tbsps
Soda bicarbonate .... 1 tsp
Lemon juice .... 1 tbsp
Mustard seeds .... 1 tsp
Coconut (scraped) .... ½ cup

METHOD OF PREPARATION

1   Take gram flour in a bowl. Add beaten yogurt and warm water. Whisk thoroughly so that no lumps remain. The mixture should be a little thick in consistency. Add salt and leave it covered to ferment for three to four hours.

2   Remove stems and wash green chillies. Peel and wash ginger. Grind green chillies and ginger into a paste.

3   Clean, wash and chop coriander leaves. When gram flour mixture has fermented, add ginger-chilli paste. Add turmeric powder and correct seasoning.

4   Heat the steamer.

5   Grease the *dhokla* mould/shallow cake tin with a little oil. In a small bowl take soda bicarbonate, one teaspoon of oil and lemon juice. Mix and add to the gram flour mixture. Whisk briskly.

6   Pour batter into the greased mould and steam for ten to twelve minutes.

7   When a little cool, cut into squares and keep in a serving bowl/plate.

8   Heat remaining oil in a small pan. Add mustard seeds. When the seeds begin to crackle, remove and pour over the *dhoklas*.

9   Serve, garnished with chopped coriander leaves and scraped coconut.

Khaman Dhokla

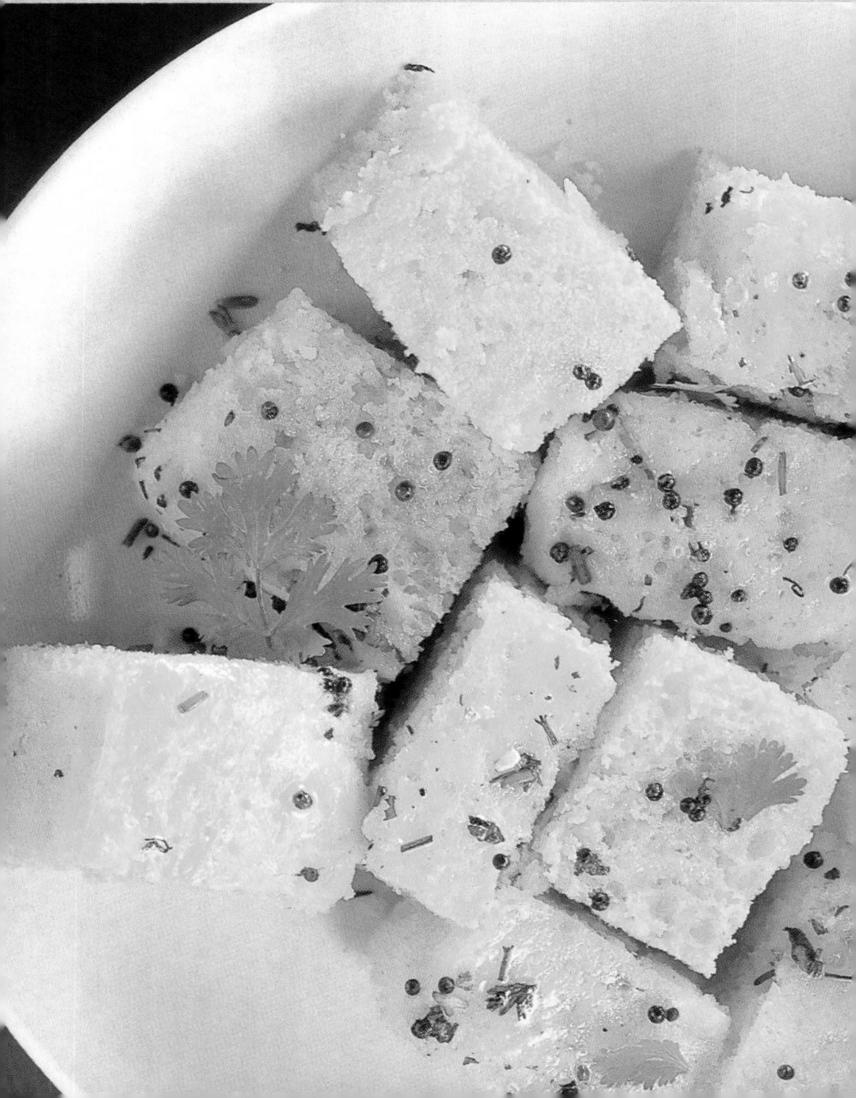

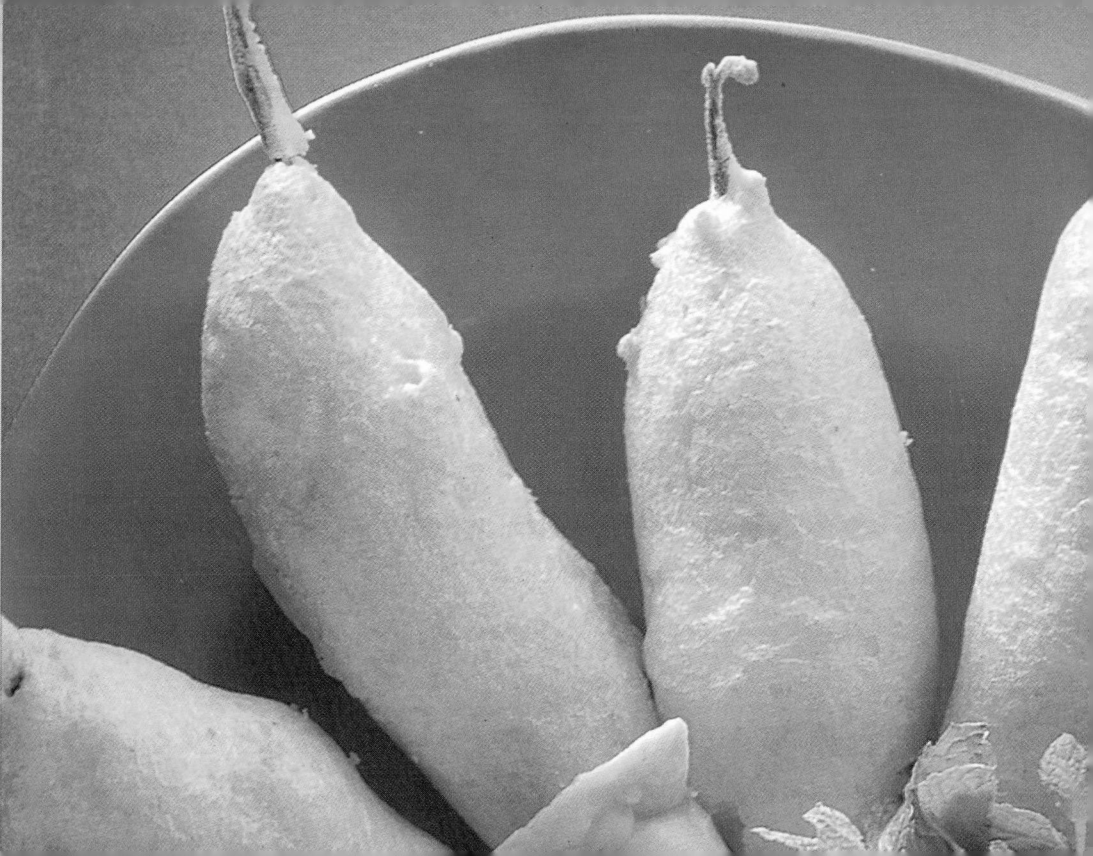

Mirchi Vada

Patra

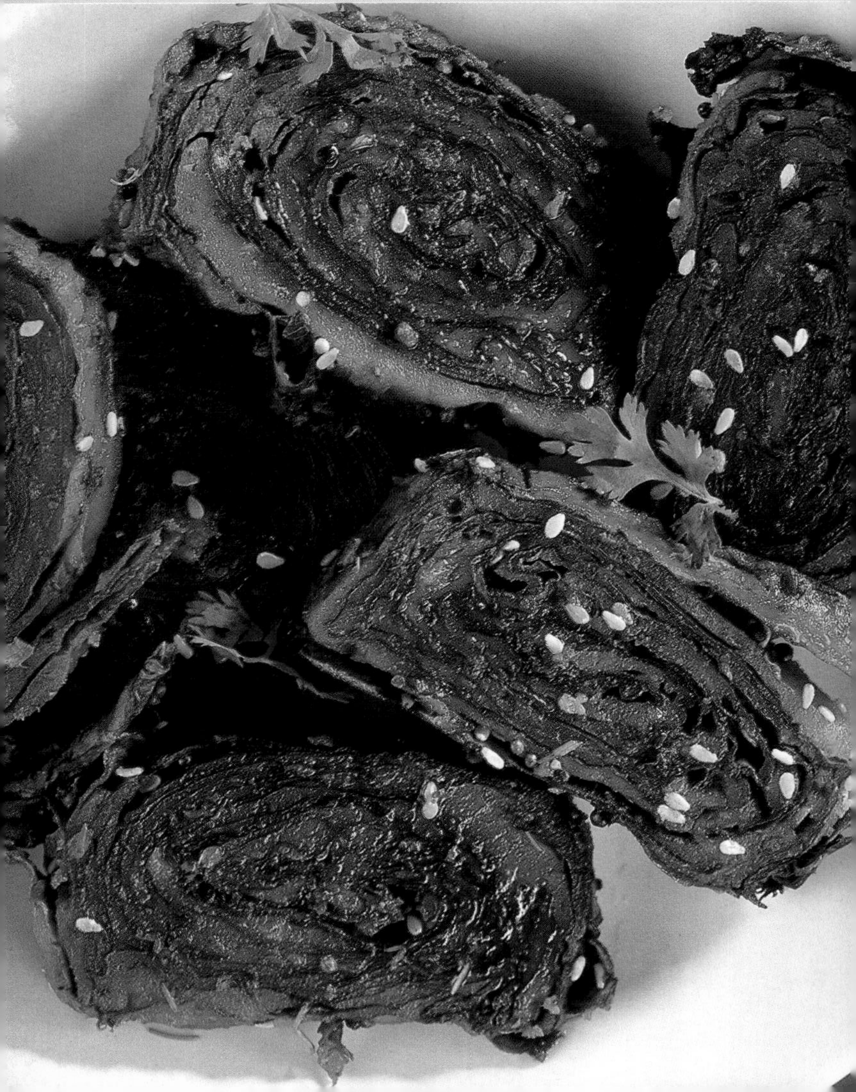

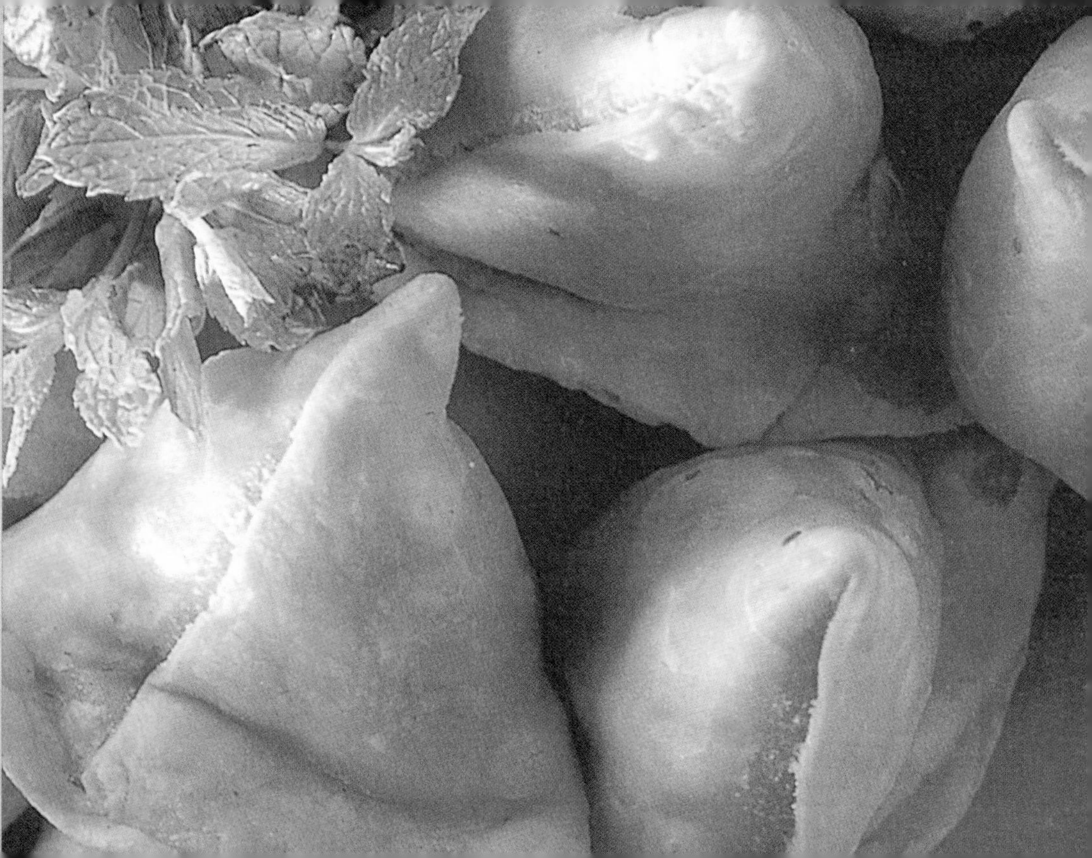

Vegetable Samosa

VEGETABLE SAMOSA

INGREDIENTS

For dough

Refined flour (*maida*) .. 1 ¾ cups
Carom seeds (*ajwain*) ...... ½ tsp
Ghee/oil .... 3 tbsps
Salt...................................... to taste

For stuffing

Green peas (shelled) .... ½ cup
Ginger .... 1 inch piece
Green chillies.............................2

Potatoes ....2 large sized
Fresh coriander leaves ... a few sprigs
Oil .... 2 tbsps + to deep-fry
Cumin seeds ....1 tsp
Red chilli powder ....1 tsp
Salt .... to taste
Dried mango powder (*amchur*)
....1 tsp
Garam masala powder ....1 tsp

METHOD OF PREPARATION

1 Sieve *maida* and mix in *ajwain*, *ghee* and salt to taste. Knead into a stiff dough adding water as required. Cover with a damp muslin cloth and keep for ten to fifteen minutes.

2   Wash green peas and cook in salted boiling water till soft. Refresh in cold water and let drain completely.

3   Peel, wash and chop ginger. Remove stems, wash and chop green chillies. Peel, wash and cut potatoes into small cubes. Clean, wash and chop coriander leaves.

4   Heat oil in a pan, add cumin seeds. As they begin to change colour, add ginger, green chillies and potato cubes. Add red chilli powder, salt, dry mango powder and *garam masala* powder. Stir well.

5   Sprinkle a little water and cook covered till potatoes are done. Add green peas and cook for five minutes on low heat. Add coriander leaves and let the mixture cool. Divide into sixteen equal portions and shape into balls,

6   Divide dough into sixteen equal portions and roll them into balls. Apply a little flour and roll them out into thin elongated discs of four-inch diameter.

7   Cut into half and apply water on the edges. Shape into a cone and stuff with potato and peas filling. Seal edges well.

8   Heat sufficient oil in a *kadai* on medium heat. Deep fry *samosas* in medium hot oil till crisp and golden brown.

9   Serve hot with tamarind *chutney*.

PATRA

INGREDIENTS

Colocassia (*arbi*) leaves 12
Gram flour (*besan*) ...... 1½ cups
Green chillies 4-5
Ginger .... 1 inch piece
Fresh coriander leaves .... a few sprigs
Coriander powder .... 2 tsps
Cumin powder .... 1 tsp
Red chilli powder .... 1 tsp
Turmeric powder .... 1 tsp

Sesame seeds .... 2 tsps
Soda bicarbonate .... ½ tsp
Salt .... to taste
Oil .... 4 tbsps
Jaggery (grated) .... 3½ tbsps
Tamarind pulp .... 2 tbsps
Mustard seeds .... 1 tsp
Asafoetida .... a pinch
Coconut (scraped) .... ¼ cup

METHOD OF PREPARATION

1 Remove the thick stems from *arbi* leaves. Wash leaves and wipe dry.
2 Remove stems and wash green chillies. Peel and wash ginger. Grind green chillies and ginger to a paste. Clean, wash and chop coriander leaves.
3 Sieve gram flour. Mix in coriander powder, cumin powder, red chilli

powder and turmeric powder. Add sesame seeds, soda bicarbonate, salt, green chilli-ginger paste, two tablespoons of oil and jaggery. Add tamarind pulp and mix well.

4   Spread the paste evenly on the back of each leaf, fold over the two sides and then roll tightly.

5   Form into six inches rolls, making sure that all the batter is inside the leaf. Place the rolls on a sieve.

6   Steam rolls for about thirty to forty minutes, or till cooked. Remove and let cool. Cut into half centimeter thick slices.

7   Heat remaining oil in a *kadai*. Add mustard seeds. When they begin to crackle, add asafoetida and add the *patra*. Sauté till golden brown.

8   Serve hot, garnished with scraped coconut and chopped coriander leaves.

STEAMED CRESCENTS

INGREDIENTS

Rice flour .... 1 cup
Salt....................................... 1 tsp
Oil... 1 tsp

Filling

Carrot .... 1 medium sized
Onion .... 1 medium sized
Garlic .... 6-8 cloves
Ginger .... 1 inch piece
Green chillies........................... 4-5

Capsicum .... 1 medium sized
Bengal gram split (*chana dal*)
(roasted) .... ¼ cup
Oil .... 1 tbsp
Cumin seeds .... ½ tsp
Onion seeds (*kalonji*) .... ½ tsp
Dried mango powder (*amchur*) .
.... 1 tsp
Salt .... to taste

METHOD OF PREPARATION

1   Peel, wash and grate carrot. Peel, wash and chop onion, garlic and
    ginger as finely as possible. Remove stems, wash and chop green
    chillies. Wash capsicum, halve, deseed and chop. Crush roasted
    chana dal lightly.

2   Heat oil in a non-stick pan, add cumin seeds and *kalonji*. Stir-fry
    briefly. Add onion, garlic, ginger and green chillies and sauté for
    three to four minutes.

3   Add capsicum and grated carrot and continue cooking. Add crushed *chana dal, amchur* and salt to taste. Remove from heat and let cool. Divide into sixteen portions.

4   Bring one cup of water to a boil in a thick-bottomed non-stick pan. Add one teaspoon of salt and oil. When water starts boiling, add rice flour in a continuous flow, stirring rapidly to avoid lumps. Cook for three to four minutes, stirring continuously.

5   Remove onto a plate, cover with a damp cloth and let it sweat for a few minutes. Knead with your palm to a smooth dough. Cover and keep aside.

6   Divide rice dough into sixteen equal portions and make them into balls.

7   Lightly oil your palm and spread each ball to approximately three inches round disc, pressing the dough with your fingers to a thin disc. Place sufficient filling and fold into a half moon shape. Press edges firmly with your fingers to seal.

8   Repeat with the rest of the dough.

9   Heat sufficient water in a steam pot and steam vegetable crescents in small batches for about ten to twelve minutes or till completely cooked.

10 Serve immediately with a hot and spicy sauce of your choice.

FOUR SEASONS PIZZA

INGREDIENTS

Pizza base .... 2 (9 inches in diameter)

For the sauce

Tomatoes .... 2 medium sized
Onion .... ½ small sized
Garlic .... 2 cloves
Fresh basil leaves 2
Oregano .... a pinch
Pepper powder .... a pinch
Olive oil .... 1 tbsp
Tomato puree .... ½ cup
Salt .... to taste

For the topping

Capsicums .... 2 medium sized
Tomatoes .... 2 medium sized
Cottage cheese (*paneer*) .... 200 gms
Fresh button mushrooms 10-12
Stuffed green olives 4-5
Stuffed black olives 4-5
Corn kernels .... ½ cup
Mozzarella cheese (grated) .... 2 cups
Red chilli flakes .... 2 tsps
Dry oregano .... ½ tsp

METHOD OF PREPARATION

For the sauce

1. Wash and quarter tomatoes. Peel, wash and chop onion. Peel, wash and chop garlic. Wash and tear basil leaves with hands.
2. Place tomatoes in two cups of boiling hot water, blanch, peel and chop finely.

3   Mix in rest of the ingredients and cook in a non-stick pan for two to three minutes on medium heat. Let cool and blend into a smooth sauce.

For the topping

4   Wash, halve and deseed capsicums. Cut into half a centimetre thick round slices.

5   Wash and cut tomatoes into half a centimetre thick round slices. Cut *paneer* into half a centimetre thick triangular slices with each side being one inch.

6   Clean, wash and thinly slice mushrooms. Thinly slice green and black olives.

For the pizza

7   Spread sauce on each pizza base. Spread half of the grated cheese equally on both. Arrange corn on one quarter of each pizza, mushroom slices on the second quarter, capsicum and tomato slices on the third quarter, *paneer* slices on the fourth quarter.

8   Sprinkle red chilli flakes, oregano and the remaining cheese. Spread the green olive slices over the *paneer* slices and black olive slices over the mushroom slices. Place on a baking tray and cook in the Grill (TOP) for ten minutes.

CHEF'S TIP

The pizza bases can be baked in advance and finishing can be done with the sauce and the topping.

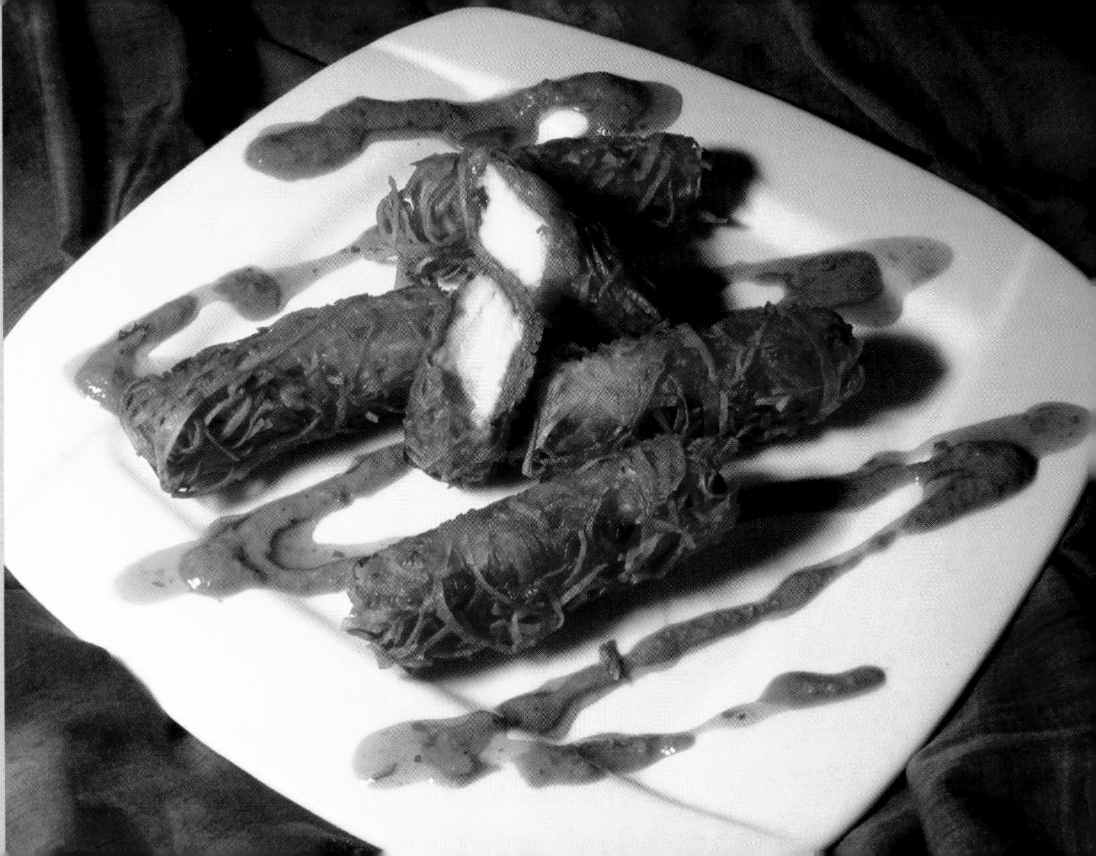

Thread Paneer

THREAD PANEER

INGREDIENTS

Cottage cheese (*paneer*) .. 250 gms
Garlic .... 6 cloves
Spring roll wrappers 6
Sweet chilli sauce .... 2 tbsps
Lemon juice .... 2 tbsps
White pepper powder .... 1 tsp
Ajinomoto .... ¼ tsp

Soy sauce .... 1 tbsp
Sugar .... 2 tsps
Salt .... to taste
Refined flour (*maida*) .... 2 tbsps
Cornstarch .... 1 tbsp
Oil .... to deep fry

METHOD OF PREPARATION

1   Cut *paneer* into two-inch long, half-inch wide and half-inch thick fingers. Wash, peel and finely chop garlic. Cut the spring roll wrappers into juliennes.

2   In a bowl mix garlic, sweet chilli sauce, lemon juice, white pepper powder, Ajinomoto, soy sauce, sugar and salt to taste. Apply this mixture liberally on *paneer* fingers and leave aside to marinate for fifteen minutes.

3   Mix in refined flour and cornstarch. Keep aside for ten minutes.
4   Spread spring roll wrapper julienne on a plate. Roll marinated *paneer* in them. Press well with your hand so that julienne stick to the *paneer*.
5   Heat sufficient oil in a wok, deep fry *paneer* fingers for two to three minutes on medium heat, turning frequently or until crisp and golden brown in colour.
6   Remove, drain onto an absorbent kitchen towel and serve hot with a sauce of your choice.

VEG OPEN SANDWICH

INGREDIENTS

Bread .... 8 slices
Spinach leaves 15-20
Onions .... 2 medium sized
Garlic .... 4 cloves
Butter .... 1 tbsp

White sauce .... ¼ cup
Cheese (grated) .... 1 cup
Salt .... to taste
White pepper powder .... ¼ tsp

METHOD OF PREPARATION

1   Grill bread slices on one side, cut them into triangles and keep aside.
2   Trim, clean, and wash spinach leaves well. Heat three cups of water to boiling point. Dip spinach leaves and drain in thirty seconds. Let cool and chop finely. Peel, wash and chop onions and garlic.
3   Heat butter in a pan, sauté onions and garlic for half a minute. Add spinach and sauté for a minute.

4   Stir in white sauce and adjust seasoning.
5   Spread mixture on plain side of bread slices. Top each with grated
    cheese and grill them in an oven or a griller till cheese melts or
    turns golden brown.
6   Serve hot with tomato ketchup.

POTATO CHAKLI

INGREDIENTS

Potatoes .... 12 medium sized
Rice flour .... ½ cup
Fresh coriander leaves ....
.... 1 medium bunch
Green chillies 6

Salt .... to taste
Sesame seeds .... 3 tsps
Ghee .... 1 tbsp
Oil .... to deep-fry

METHOD OF PREPARATION

1 Wash and boil potatoes. Cool and peel.
2 Clean and wash coriander leaves. Remove stems, wash and chop green chillies.
3 Make a smooth paste of coriander leaves and green chillies using a little salt.

4   Mash potatoes well and knead into a dough adding coriander-green chilli paste and rice flour.

5   Add sesame seeds and adjust salt. Mix well.

6   Apply a little *ghee* on your palms and shape dough into a smooth ball.

7   Break off portions and place in *sev* maker, which has the star (*chakli*) plate.

8   Gently press out spirals on small pieces of paper.

9   Heat sufficient oil in a *kadai* till moderately hot.

10 Drop *chaklis* one by one and fry till golden and crisp.

11 Drain onto an absorbent paper. Cool and store in an air-tight container.

STUFFED MUSHROOMS

INGREDIENTS

Fresh button mushrooms ....
.... 16 medium sized
Cottage cheese (crumbled) .. ¼ cup
Processed cheese (grated) ..... ¼ cup
Onion .... 1 medium sized
Garlic .... 4-5 cloves

Butter .... 5 tbsps
Salt .... to taste
White pepper powder .... ¼ tsp
Nutmeg powder .... ¼ tsp
Lemon juice .... 1 tbsp

METHOD OF PREPARATION

1 Remove stalks of mushrooms, clean and wash well and chop finely.
   Keep aside.
2 Clean the heads of mushrooms, wash and wipe dry and prepare it
   for stuffing.
3 Peel, wash and chop onion and garlic.

4   Heat three tablespoons of butter in a non-stick pan and add onion and garlic. Sauté for a minute and add mushroom stalks and salt to taste. Continue to cook for a minute.

5   Add cottage cheese and white pepper powder and mix it well. Add processed cheese and nutmeg powder.

6   Stuff this mixture into mushroom heads and sandwich two of such together, holding them with a toothpick.

7   Smear the remaining butter and lemon juice on mushrooms. Preheat oven to 175°C. Place mushrooms in a baking tray and bake at 175° C for seven to eight minutes. Serve hot.

RED COLESLAW IN PITA POCKETS

INGREDIENTS

Pita bread .... 4 medium sized
Red cabbage ..... ½ medium sized
Onions .... 2 small sized
Red radishes 2
Red apples .... 2 medium sized

Lemon juice .... 1 tbsp
Low fat cheese spread ..... 3 tbsps
Skimmed milk yogurt ..... 3 tbsps
Salt .... to taste
Pepper powder .... ½ tsp

METHOD OF PREPARATION

1   Wash, trim, remove core and shred cabbage. Peel, wash and thinly slice onions and radishes.
2   Wash, peel, core and grate apples. Mix cabbage, onions, radishes, apples and lemon juice in a bowl.
3   Add cheese spread, skimmed milk yogurt, salt and pepper. Mix well. Divide red coleslaw into eight equal portions.
4   Warm the pita breads on a griddle plate or alternatively in a preheated oven at 160 °C for five minutes. Cut each pita bread into two and fill each half with a portion of red coleslaw.
5   Serve with a sauce or *chutney* of your choice.

WADA
PAV

INGREDIENTS

Potatoes .... 4-6 medium sized
Pav bread 8
Green chillies 4
Garlic .... 8-10 cloves
Fresh coriander leaves ....
.... ¼ medium bunch
Lemon 1
Turmeric powder .... ¼ tsp
Salt .... to taste
Asafoetida .... a pinch
For batter
Gram flour *(besan)* ...... 1¼ cups
Salt .... to taste

Red chilli powder .... ½ tsp
Turmeric powder .... ¼ tsp
Soda bicarbonate ..... a small pinch
Oil .... 1 tbsp + for deep-frying
Red chutney
Dry coconut *(khopra)* (grated) ..
.... 3 tbsps
Red chilli powder .... 2 tsps
Garlic .... 4-6 cloves
Oil .... 1 tbsp
Gram flour crumbs *(besan boondi)*
.... ½ cup
Salt .... to taste

METHOD OF PREPARATION

1 Wash, boil, cool, peel and roughly mash potatoes.
2 Peel and wash garlic. Remove stems and wash green chillies. Grind garlic and green chillies to a paste. Clean, wash and chop coriander leaves. Squeeze lemon to extract the juice.
3 Mix together potatoes, garlic-green chilli paste, turmeric powder, asafoetida, lemon juice, chopped coriander leaves and salt.
4 Divide into eight equal portions and shape into balls. Keep aside.
5 Place *besan* in a bowl, add soda bicarbonate, turmeric powder, red chilli powder and salt. Heat one tablespoon of oil and add it to *besan* mixture. Mix well and make a coating consistency batter using water as required.
6 To make red *chutney*, peel and wash garlic. Grind together grated dry coconut, red chilli powder and garlic. Heat oil in a pan and add this mixture to it and sauté for a minute, add *besan boondi* and mix well. Remove from heat and season with salt.
7 Heat sufficient oil in a *kadai*. Dip potato mixture balls in batter and deep fry in hot oil till golden brown in colour. Remove and drain onto an absorbent kitchen towel.

8   Slit *pav* breads horizontally not slicing them completely. Spread a little of the red chutney on inner sides of the *pav* and stuff it with hot *wadas*. Serve hot.

CHEF'S TIP

For the red chutney save gram flour crumbs *(besan boondis)* obtained during the frying of *wadas*. Remove excess oil and allow it to cool.

CRISPY WONTONS

INGREDIENTS

Wonton skins	16
Onion	1 medium sized
Garlic	1 clove
Ginger	½ inch piece
Fresh button mushrooms	4-5 medium sized
Oil	1 tbsp + to deep-fry
Salt	to taste

Sauce

Oil	2 tbsps
Spring onions	2
Red chilli	1
Green chilli	1
Light soy sauce	3 tbsps
Vinegar	1 tbsp
Dry sherry	1 tbsp
Sugar	a pinch

METHOD OF PREPARATION

1 Peel, wash and finely chop onion, garlic and ginger. Clean and wash mushrooms thoroughly and finely chop.
2 For sauce, trim, wash and chop spring onions. Remove stem, wash, slit, deseed and chop red chilli and green chilli.

3   Heat one tablespoon of oil in a preheated wok or frying pan.

4   Add onion, garlic and ginger and stir-fry for two minutes. Stir in mushrooms and fry for further two minutes. Season well with salt and leave to cool.

5   Place one teaspoon of the cooled mushroom filling in the centre of each wonton skin.

6   Bring two opposite corners of each wonton skin together to cover the mixture and pinch together to seal. Repeat with remaining corners.

7   Heat sufficient oil in a large saucepan. Deep-fry wontons in batches until golden and crisp. Do not overheat oil or wontons will brown on the outside before they are properly cooked inside. Remove wontons and drain onto an absorbent kitchen paper.

8   To make the sauce, heat oil in a small saucepan until quite hot or until a small cube of bread dropped in oil browns in a few seconds. Put spring onions and chillies in a bowl and pour hot oil slowly on top. Mix in light soy sauce, vinegar, dry sherry and sugar.

9   Transfer crispy wontons to a serving dish and serve with the dipping sauce.

CRUNCHY PANEER PAKORA

INGREDIENTS

Cottage cheese (*paneer*) ... 250 gms
Oil .... to deep fry
Boondi .... 1 cup

For garlic *chutney*
Garlic .... 8-10 cloves
Oil .... 1 tsp
Red chilli powder .... 1 tbsp
Salt .... to taste

For batter
Gram flour (*besan*) .... 1 cup
Garlic .... 1½ inch piece
Ginger .... 5 cloves
Red chilli powder .... 1 tsp
Turmeric powder .... ½ tsp
Soda bicarbonate .... a pinch
Salt .... to taste

METHOD OF PREPARATION

1 Wash and cut cottage cheese into two inch by half inch by half inch sized batons. Slit each baton into half leaving one edge intact for filling.

2   Crush *boondi* with your hand and keep aside.

3   To make garlic *chutney*, peel and roast garlic in one teaspoon of oil. Mix with red chilli powder and salt and grind to a smooth paste.

4   To prepare batter, peel and wash ginger and garlic and grind together to make a paste. Mix gram flour with this paste, red chilli powder, turmeric powder, soda bicarbonate and salt. Add sufficient water and whisk well to make a batter of a coating consistency. Rest the batter for about fifteen minutes.

5   Stuff garlic chutney into the slit of each cottage cheese baton.

6   Heat sufficient oil in a *kadai*, dip each baton of cottage cheese into the batter, roll in the crushed *boondi* and deep fry on medium heat till crisp and golden brown.

7   Serve hot with a *chutney* of your choice.

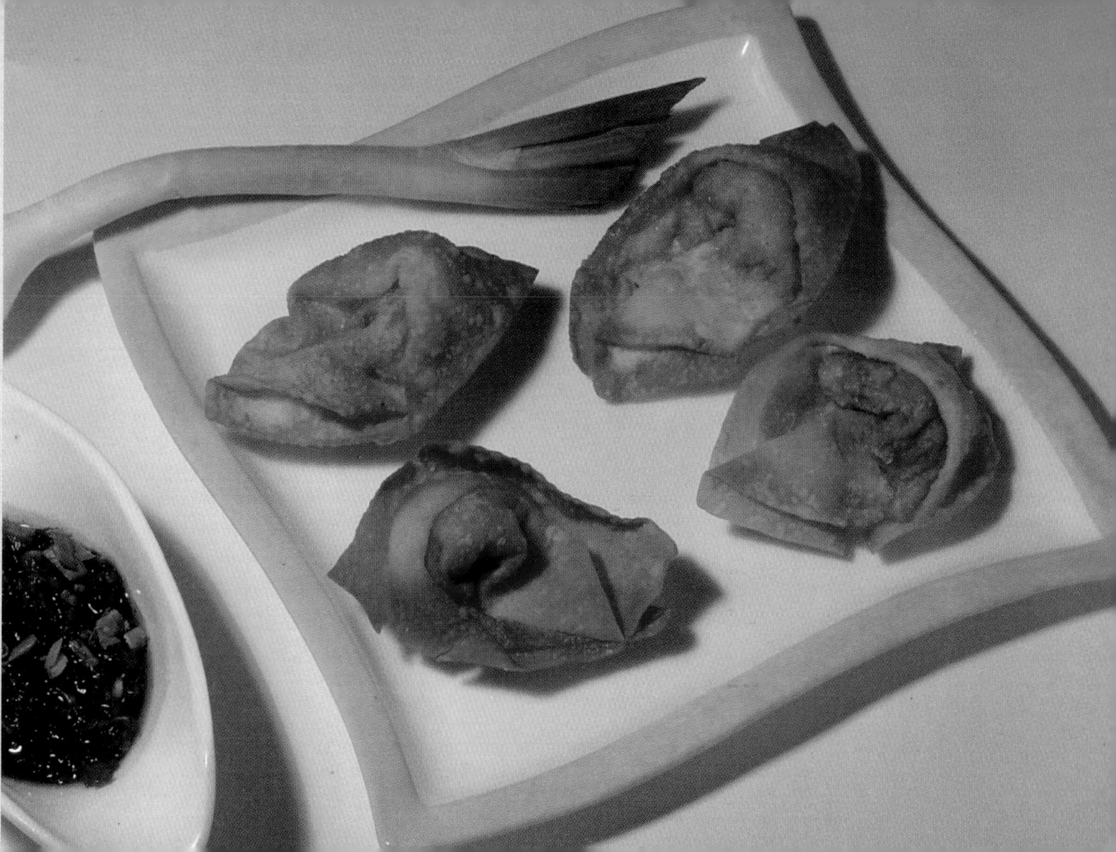

Crispy Wontons